FINDING OUR WAY

Also by John Kater

A Faith for Teenagers

FINDING
OUR WAY

American Christians
in Search of
the City of God

Lessons from Panama

John L. Kater Jr.

COWLEY PUBLICATIONS
Cambridge, Massachusetts

Published in the United States of America by Cowley Publications, a division of the Society of St. John the Evangelist. No portion of this book may be reproduced, stored in or introduced into a retrieval system, or transmitted, in any form or by any means—including photocopying—without the prior written permission of Cowley Publications, except in the case of brief quotations embodied in critical articles and reviews.

International Standard Book Number: 1-56101-029-4
Library of Congress Number: 91-6679

Library of Congress Cataloging-in-Publication Data

Kater, John.

Finding our way / John L. Kater, Jr.

p. cm.

Includes bibliographical references.

ISBN 1-56101-029-4

1. Sociology, Christian—United States. 2. Christianity and justice—United States. 3. United States—Church history—20th century. 4. Social justice—Biblical teaching.

I. Title.

BR526.K38 1991

277.3—dc20   91-6679

This book is printed on acid-free paper and was produced in the United States of America.

Cowley Publications
28 Temple Place
Boston, MA 02111

For the People of the Episcopal Diocese of Panama
guides and companions
on the way to God's city

ACKNOWLEDGMENTS

Many of the issues I address in this book have concerned me for many years, and have formed the subject matter of my study, teaching, and reflection for as long as I can remember. However, it was when the Bishop of Panama, the Rt. Rev. James H. Ottley, invited me in 1984 to join his staff as Education Officer that I found myself in a setting that enabled me to test the reality of what I had previously studied from a distance. The theologians who are rediscovering the church's faith in the Latin American context provided me with ideas; my ministry in Panama gave me the chance to test them in practice.

I am grateful to Bishop Ottley, Glenda McQueen, Maiziee Lennan, Julio Murray, and all my friends and colleagues of the Diocese of Panama who have consistently answered my questions, corrected my errors, challenged my assumptions, and encouraged my reflections. The catechists of the Diocese of Panama's rural missions suppose that they were my students, but the truth is that they taught me far more about the subject matter of these pages.

I am also grateful to the Episcopal Church for their support during a three-month furlough in 1987 in which I wrote an initial draft of this book. Cynthia Shattuck of Cowley Publications has (as usual) been a wise, demanding, and supportive editor. Her quiet insistence that I anchor my ideas firmly in the real world has, I hope, resulted in a more accessible and human work. Its readability was also improved by the numerous suggestions made by Stephen Perry, to whom I am appreciative for his patient and careful review of later versions of the text.

Unless otherwise noted, all biblical quotations are taken from the New Revised Standard Version.

John L. Kater
Panama City

TABLE OF CONTENTS

INTRODUCTION

O nce upon a time, Christians understood their faith in terms of a journey. They believed they were following in the footsteps of their ancestors towards a land they had never seen. They had a firm vision of their destination, and approached the journey required of them with enthusiasm and zeal. They understood the hardships on their way as incidental, of little importance, and surely to be forgotten in the joy that awaited them at their journey's end.

Their goal was nothing less than the City of God.

The people we meet in the pages of the New Testament were inspired by their certainty that God's city would rise up to meet them and reveal that their labors had not been in vain. For many centuries, that hope survived to give meaning to generations of their descendants.

No one embraced the imagery of that journey and its goal more fervently than American Christians. Perhaps their fervor stemmed from their own origins. Most Christians on the North American continent have a story to tell of the journey by which their ancestors found themselves in America.

The first Christians in America were Spanish, zealously promoting their Roman Catholicism among peoples whose very existence was a recent discovery. Further north, British settlers in New England found themselves confronting the wilderness much as the Hebrews, whom they took as their model, had struggled to make themselves at home in the Promised Land. Black Christians, whose arrival in this hemisphere was under far different circumstances, nevertheless embraced the theme of the journey as the process by which they expected to be saved—at the hour of death, surely, but also from the slavery to which they were subjected but never accustomed.

Those various ancestors of many of today's Americans lived by different dreams, and painted their hopes in radically distinct images. They would no doubt have surprised each other if they had discovered that all considered themselves travelers on a journey—perhaps even pilgrims. But the truth is, they all would have described themselves as on the way to a promise and a destination that remained in the future and gave meaning and direction to their lives. In that shared imagery, they were acting out the heritage of their biblical ancestors in faith. Indeed, American culture was shaped in large part through the Bible's imagery of hope and destination. The City of God, however it was defined, was a real and living goal for generations of American Christians. It gave purpose to their life and death. They sought it as an earthly model and as their final heavenly destination.

But no more. The once vivid imagery and the eager expectation of the City of God have lost their power. The city's reality as a living symbol has faded. The image of the journey, which formerly conveyed a sense of purpose, direction, and destiny, no longer moves American -Christians.

If we persist in the image of the journey at all, we are more apt to use it as a metaphor for transition. We are painfully conscious of the abrupt changes and tumultuous passages we encounter: ruptures in the family, economic upheavals, medical revelations with frightening consequences, unexpected brushes with violence. These are the moments when we recall that we lack ultimate stability and rootedness. Such occasions are thrust upon us and we respond to them without joy; certainly we do not perceive ourselves as pilgrims. This is no journey of faith, but the risky maneuvering of an obstacle course not of our choosing. We congratulate ourselves if we can move across town or across the country with no more than our share of calamities. It rarely occurs to us that God might be involved in these transitions. God, we believe, has to do with being at rest and peace.

What happened? How did we American Christians, who once prided ourselves on taking the scriptures so seriously, lose our way? How did a people who once modeled their lives on the journey towards God's city come to lose their sense of destination? What were the effects of that loss on a faith meant for people on the move? Are we lost forever? Can we find our way?

I undertake the search for the answers to these questions with considerable urgency. I am convinced that Christian faith is really a way of living with shared expectations that God's hope for us can come true—or, to put it another way, that the City of God is real. I believe that it was in the service of that hope that Jesus lived and died. I believe that hope was strengthened beyond measure when God raised him from the dead. I believe that hope once transformed the world and can continue to turn the world upside down in a process that will also renew our own dreams. That hope is largely unknown to Christians in the United States today, but in other settings the City of God is a dynamic goal that animates and challenges. I am convinced that the rebirth of our faith depends upon rediscovering that vision, and once more finding our way toward the City of God.

Chapter 1
THE BIRTH OF A VISION

I *t had been a long, hard crossing. The Arabella, its sails
straining against the winds of the Atlantic, its timbers
washed by waves that towered over the groaning decks,
had faltered more than once. Its passengers had found their
faith tried by the imminent possibility of death. But they had
survived, and now the Arabella was lying just off the Massachusetts coast. The year was 1630; ten years had already
passed since the first settlers had stepped onto the shore at Ply-
mouth.*

*On board the Arabella were a number of people who had
come to swell the population of this forlorn outpost. Among
them was John Winthrop, the first governor of the Massachusetts Bay Colony. As he sat on deck, waiting to set foot in a
new world, his heart pounding with anticipation, he wrote these
words:*

> *Thus stands the cause between God and us: we are entered
> into covenant with Him for this work.... We shall find that the
> God of Israel is among us, when ten of us shall be able to re-
> sist a thousand of our enemies, when He shall make us a
> praise and glory, that men of succeeding generations shall
> say, 'The Lord make it like that of New England.' For we
> must consider that we shall be as a City upon a Hill, the eyes
> of all people are upon us....* [1]

Probably almost everyone on board the *Arabella* shared not only Winthrop's enthusiasm, but his sense of *mission* and *destiny* as well. Heirs of a religious tradition that took the Bible with absolute seriousness, they had no doubt they were acting out once again the story of the Hebrews as they made their way to the Promised Land. Crossing the Atlantic Ocean aboard a tiny vessel like the *Arabella* seemed to them every bit as miraculous as the Israelites' crossing of the Red Sea. The American shores appeared as prosperous as Canaan, rich with the promise of untold abundance. And the sea divided them from the old world, the past with its dangers and threats, as sharply as it had once put a barrier between the Hebrews and their slavery.

To Winthrop and countless others who made their way to the colonies with hearts full of hope, this continent was indeed God's Promised Land, and they were the new "chosen people." Their mission was to be a "light to the nations," a people who would become what the Bible told them Israel had never been: a society that lived out God's commandments. And just as the Hebrews trusted that God would reward their obedience with blessings, so these new Americans confidently expected to prosper by keeping God's laws. The Bible served as their guide, not only for showing how God meant humankind to live together, but also for interpreting their own story.

Americans are certainly not the only people who have sought to understand their history in the light of God's purposes. But few have ever tried so consciously to model their story after the biblical story, or worked so hard to copy the values and priorities of an ancient people when they established and evaluated their national life.

Like biblical Israel, Americans understood themselves to be a *covenant community*. Certainly John Winthrop and his companions founded their settlements with a firm sense that they were bound to each other and to God in the doing. They recalled that when God delivered the Hebrews from their slavery in Egypt, the people pledged themselves to God by that most solemn of commitments, a *covenant*.

Israel's life as a people was defined by that covenant, summarized by the prophet Jeremiah: "You shall be my people, and I will be your God" (Jer. 30:22). Trusting God's commitment to them, Israel joyfully promised to worship no other. The covenant was summarized in (though not limited to) what came to be called the "Decalogue"—the Ten Commandments.

But their covenant with God also spelled out the Israelites' relationships with one another as a chosen people. These commandments form the heart of a truly remarkable conception of a nation that has come into being as a result of its bond with God. The community that shares the covenant is held together by principles of mutual respect comprising a rudimentary, but highly effective, form of *justice*. Most importantly, Israel's ethical behavior—how its members treat one another—is understood as part of its duty to God. The God who brought the chosen people out of slavery now requires that they show respect precisely by respecting one another.

This same sense of commitment to community lay behind the formation of the United States as an independent nation. We catch something of the power of that covenant in Thomas Jefferson's conclusion to the Declaration of Independence: "And for the support of this declaration, with a firm reliance on the protection of divine providence, we mutually pledge to each other our lives, our fortunes, and our sacred honor." This pledge of mutual support and commitment helped Americans survive an environment that was often hostile and always challenging. The imagery of life on the frontier underlines the ways in which Americans considered themselves to be part of a community. If barn-raisings and quilting parties have become part of our national folklore, it is because survival demanded that people help each other. But at every moment, God was the unseen partner who held the bonds together.

Not only is the basic sense of national identity rooted in a covenant with God, but the very institutions of American society are considered to be God-given. What impelled people like John Winthrop and many of the original colonists who came to America was the search for a setting in which they could practice the politics they believed were in accordance with God's rule. They knew well the claims of the monarchy that the king ruled by "divine right," claims supported by a state church that was an integral part of the royal establishment. But they rejected those claims, and with them the church that supprted them. Their reading of Scripture brought them to different conclusions. They longed for the opportunity to set up a "commonwealth" in which they could organize society as they believed God wanted it.

The documents by which the founders of this nation expressed their political beliefs and formulated their institutions— the Declaration of Independence and the Constitution—reveal that they also believed their work was in obedience to God's will as revealed in both Nature and Scripture. In this sense, they were the heirs of the first colonists, even when they did not share their church allegiance. "Preserve your government with the utmost attention and solicitude," one preacher told the General Court of New Hampshire on the eve of the 1788 elections; "it is the remarkable gift of heaven." Popular Christianity has continued to affirm that the "American way of life" is established on biblical norms. "I am positive in my belief regarding the Constitution," Jerry Falwell wrote in 1980, "that God led in the development of that document.... Our Founding Fathers established America's laws and precepts on the prin-

8

ciples recorded in the laws of God, including the Ten Commandments."[2]

Why should the American people be singled out to enter into such a special covenant relationship with God? For Winthrop and countless others, the answer lies in the *divine mission* that has been entrusted to them, focused in the image of the "city upon a hill." Winthrop borrowed the image itself from Matthew's gospel:

> You are the light of the world. A city set on a hill cannot be hid. No one after lighting a lamp puts it under a basket, but on the lampstand, and it gives light to all in the house. Let your light so shine before others, that they may see your good works and give glory to your Father in heaven. (Matt. 5:14-16)

In its original context, Jesus used the image of the city on a hill to remind his hearers that since public behavior reveals the values and beliefs that motivate them, his followers should act in such a way as to commend their faith. John Winthrop applied it to the little band that was venturing forth to create a new society, based on their reading of God's purposes. As God's "chosen people," Winthrop warned them they would be watched by the whole world; they are called, then, to live in such a way that their insights and accomplishments will inspire the rest of the world's peoples.

This sense of mission is rarely absent from the American national consciousness. The generation responsible for the independence of the United States certainly understood that their efforts would serve as an example to the world. "This great American revolution...will be attended to and contemplated by all nations," proclaimed Yale president Ezra Stiles in 1783.

> May the general goverment of these United States, when established, appear to be the best which the nations have yet known...and may the everlasting Gospel diffuse its Heavenly

> light and spread Righteousness, Liberty, and Peace
> throughout the world,

prayed the preacher Samuel Langdon a few years later.

Early in this century, Indiana's senator Albert J. Beveridge demonstrated well the survival of this sense of national vocation (and the arrogance that often accompanies it) when he declared:

> God has given [the English-speaking and Teutonic peoples] the spirit of progress to overwhelm the forces of reaction throughout the world.... He has made us adept in government that we may administer government among savage and senile peoples. Were it not for such a force as this the world would relapse into barbarism and night. And of all our race He has marked the American people as His chosen nation to finally lead in the redemption of the world.

Such a rationale had permitted the first settlers to conquer the land occupied by the indigenous peoples of the continent, and in the guise of "manifest destiny" it led the nation to expand from ocean to ocean. Surely it is that sense of mission, a kind of national "noblesse oblige," that enabled the imposition of American culture, economics, and politics on nations around the world, from the Philippines to Puerto Rico.

In their zeal to share the values they held dear, many Americans forgot that those values mean nothing if they are not freely chosen, and that they can be expressed in structures very different from those developed through the years by the United States. The tendency to assume that Americans are God's vanguard, in the service of the best civilization has to offer, glorifies the very concept of "progress" and gives it a religious interpretation.

Like the biblical story that shaped it, American history has been directed towards the future and the fulfillment of promises ahead on the horizon. Even as the new nation was establishing itself with a population of fewer than a million, Ezra Stiles was looking forward to the time when "this will become a great people":

> It is probable that within a century from our independence the sun will shine on fifty million of inhabitants in the United States. This will be a great, a very great nation.

As the nation has grown in economic and political power through the last three centuries, many people have intrepreted this "success" as a sign that God's will is in fact being accomplished. They tend to assume that the basic structures we live by are "givens," perhaps in need of tinkering to improve their efficiency, but right and proper in their foundations. "Most of what was bad in our present condition was worse two hundred years ago, or one hundred years ago," wrote the Congregationalist pastor Washington Gladden in 1908. It is a judgment with which most Americans, at most moments in our history, would tend to agree.

The biblical themes that have informed the American sense of identity since the nation's beginnings—covenant and mission, progress and destiny—add a unique flavor to our culture and our religion. Robert Bellah argues that, taken together, they form an important part of our "civil religion," beliefs that have "played a crucial role in the development of American institutions" and have survived into our time as a shared "set of beliefs, symbols and rituals."[3]

But the roots of those beliefs ultimately lie neither in the experience of the first colonists, nor in the soil of the New World to which they came. Rather, they are embedded in the tradition of the Bible, and especially in the hope that moved and sustained the first followers of a Jewish preacher named Jesus.

The heart of his preaching was that God's will for humankind would transform the world into something that had never been, and that living by that promise would make us new people, truly human for the first time. The long shadow of that message moved many of our ancestors to build a different kind of community in the American setting.

If we are to understand the place of faith and hope in the American dream, we must first seek out its origins in the pages of the biblical story.

QUESTIONS FOR REFLECTION

1. What strikes you as the principal characteristics of a *covenant* as understood in the Bible and by the founders of this nation?

2. Does this concept of *covenant* still survive among the American people? In what ways?

3. The founders of this country considered that its institutions and its destiny were God-given. Do you agree? What do you believe is special about being an American?

4. Do you agree with Washington Gladden's comment that "most of what is bad in our present condition was worse two hundred years ago, or one hundred years ago"? What does "progress" mean to you?

Chapter 2
THE KINGDOM IS COMING!, THE
KINGDOM IS COMING!

*T*he bright morning sky shone back from the river, blue
and cloudless. The current was sluggish, and the
stones on the bottom were clearly visible even from
the shore. The sun cast crisp shadows; though the hour was
early, people were already wishing for a bit of shade. But the
landscape was treeless, its arid emptiness suggesting that the
desert was nearby.

In the light of the sun, the speaker's eyes shone fire. His
figure was lean, hard, the muscles tense as he spoke. Spectators
gasped when they caught their first glimpse of him; he had
clothed himself in animal skins, and it was said he ate nothing
but locusts and honey from the wild. The words flowed from the
man's mouth as if he were ridding himself of an intolerable burden. He spoke of God, the God of his people who once had
freed them when they were slaves in Egypt. He recalled the
wonder of the covenant by which these people had been bound
forever to God. And he spoke of the ways in which those people
had failed their God.

Now, he assured them, God was about to act once again
on behalf of the people. For centuries their prophets had been
promising that they were not forgotten; just as they had been set
free from their slavery, God would once again intervene to
make things right. The time was near—very near—when God's

will would be fulfilled, and justice would finally come to the earth. God at last would reign over the people.

But how could they bear to encounter such a God, corrupt as they were? How could they face that justice unless they turned their lives towards God?

People seldom knew what to make of John the Baptist. Word had spread; large numbers had made the trip from Jerusalem to see what was happening down by the Jordan River. Some were offended by his words; others pretended to be amused and ridiculed the way he dressed as if he himself were one of the prophets from times past. But many were touched by his message, and the earnestness with which he called them to look at themselves in the light of God's promises and demands. When he invited them to change the course of their lives and commit themselves to the God who would soon be among them as their king and judge, they followed him into the river and allowed themselves to be thrust under its waters. They emerged with the sense of starting over and a renewed bond with God. And they gave thanks for the man named John who had given them a new beginning and a new direction.

At first, he held back. Few of the people who listened to John dared to get too near, lest they find themselves singled out as the object of his attention. But as John went on speaking about what God meant for the people, he found himself edging closer. He was fascinated, drawn by the man himself and most of all by his words.

He was a long way from home. Nazareth, the Galilean village where he had spent all his young life, lay far to the north. His family, his carpentry, his dreams, seemed to belong to a different age, a different world. John's words made sense, and they awoke in him an overwhelming longing to commit himself to God's promises. He found himself following John into the water. His life, and with it the history of the human race, was about to change forever.

Mark's gospel—his retelling of the "good news" about Jesus—begins not with the story of Jesus' conception and birth, but with his encounter with John the Baptist. Indeed, in Mark's opinion, John's appearance on the scene is itself "the beginning of the good news about Jesus the Messiah, the Son of God" (Mark 1:1).

Mark describes Jesus' baptism as the moment when his identity is made clear. It is the time when God reveals that this young man, previously unnoticed, is in fact "my Son, the beloved; with you I am well pleased" (1:11). A period of temptation in the wilderness and John's arrest set the stage for the beginning of his ministry. Everything is now ready for Jesus to begin his work.

How does Mark decribe the beginning of that ministry? "Jesus came into Galilee, proclaiming the good news of the kingdom of God, and declaring, 'The time is fulfilled, and the kingdom of God has come near'" (Mark 1:14-15).

It is clear to anyone who reads Mark's gospel that Jesus' proclamation of God's reign—or, in the terminology of that era, the "kingdom of God"—forms the heart of his message. It is equally obvious to a reader of the Bible that it was not just a theme that Jesus invented from his own imagination or experience; on the contrary, it was an image that carried enormous weight for his people. When Jesus announced that the kingdom of God was drawing near, people assumed they knew what he was talking about.

Twenty centuries later, many people who are quite at home with much of what Jesus said and did nevertheless find this aspect of his preaching alien and unfamiliar. Yet what Jesus said about God's reign was not an aside or an irrelevance. As Mark's gospel sees it, what Jesus had to say about God's kingdom was in fact the good news he offered. If that is true, we cannot grasp his message as *gospel*—as good news—unless we understand what he had to say about the reign of God. If that message is the very starting point of his teaching, ignoring it will distort and obscure the whole of Jesus' message. Trying to follow Christ without a clear sense of his destination, we will surely find ourselves lost.

Fortunately, the resouces for finding our way remain for us in the Bible. That was, after all, where Jesus and his followers found them in the first place.

As a faithful Jew, Jesus read the signs of his own times in the light of the traditions that were preserved and handed down in the Scriptures of his people. It is there we will find what we need to grasp more fully the heart of his message: "The kingdom of God is near at hand."

Jesus' teaching about the reign of God is rooted in the Jewish belief that as a people they were special and unique. That uniqueness was expressed in the way their life as a community was related to God. At a time in history when religion was customarily focused on the natural processes of life—sexuality, fertility, and the cycle of the seasons—the Hebrew people understood their God in very different terms. Not that they failed to identify the richness of the natural world as the gift of a good and attentive God, but they did not seek, or claim to find, their God primarily in nature. Rather, they pointed to their own story as the best place for finding and meeting God. Who is God? It is God who brought our ancestors out of slavery in Egypt, when they thought they had been abandoned and forgotten.

That mighty act of deliverance came to be the most important thing the Hebrews could say about their God. From their awareness of their debt to such a God came their belief that this God and this people Israel were bound together for all time. Israel was set apart from its neighbors by accepting a rigorous code of behavior, a code dictating how they were to live as a covenant people within a relationship with God. Israel bound itself to the God who had set them free, and to no other. Their great festival of remembering—the Passover, the celebration of the Exodus—meant that no one would ever forget the first and most important thing they believed about God: "I am the Lord your God, who brought you out of the land of Egypt, out of the house of slavery" (Exod. 20:2).

The covenant with God determined the nature of how the people of Israel related to one another. The God who brought them out of slavery demands that they respect and care for one another. The complex laws that make up the heritage of Israel are based on the fact that this God of freedom now demands *justice*. Furthermore, that justice is understood from the beginning as part of Israel's obligation towards God; there is no discontinuity between the commandments dictating how to behave towards God, and those commanding solicitude for the stranger, care for the poor, and a commitment to the well-being of the people as a whole. All are understood as the obligation of a people who have pledged themselves to God.

In Jesus' time, Jewish national identity was primarily a question of living within that covenant, often focused on the most visible signs it imposed. These were the Sabbath-day rest as a form of honoring God; a complex set of dietary laws, which had the effect of making sure that Jews remembered they were a people set apart; and circumcision, the physical sign that each Jewish male became part of the community he had inherited from his ancestors. But the heart of the Torah, the Law that was believed to come from Moses himself, was the demand to live as a people with justice and compassion.

How else can we interpret the complicated procedure spelled out in Leviticus 25 for coping with times when real-life situations get in the way of the ideal of justice? The Book of Leviticus attempts to provide a way of putting things right again with the "Year of Jubilee." Every fifty years, property that had been sold to satisfy its owner's debts is to be returned to its original owner; individuals who have sold themselves into slavery are to be given their freedom. Neither slavery nor property sales can ever be regarded as final. In short, twice each century there is to be a time of restoration, when conditions of inequality (for it is a fact that some people flourish while others fail) are put right again. Slavery is in fact *temporary* servitude; property sales are in reality limited-term leases. No condition of inequality is permitted to endure. In the eyes of the covenant, such inequality would violate the norm of justice that is the purpose of the Torah.

Most historians doubt that the high principles of justice supposed by the Jubilee Year were ever practised. That should not surprise us. The Jewish Scriptures paint a relentlessly honest picture of failure and denial alongside the ideals of the covenant. Even as the Egyptian army lay behind them on the far side of the Red Sea, the people were wishing they had never left the comfortable certainties of their old ways. Harsh slavery seemed more bearable than the unknown future, following a God towards a land they had never even seen.

"You shall be my people, and I will be your God." Long years later, Jeremiah summed up Israel's sense of itself as he spoke in God's name of the covenant that gave them their identity as a people. It was to be a "holy nation," not because its people were more virtuous or saintly than others, but because they understood God to be their ultimate ruler and authority.

What does it mean to be a nation dedicated to God? The psalms indicate that even when Israel had become a well-established state, with kings and armies, the people still understood that

> The Lord is King;
> he is robed in majesty;
> the Lord is robed,
> he is girded with strength (Ps. 93:1).

The king who occupies the throne in Jerusalem, whatever his personal traits and the degree of splendor his court achieves, nevertheless rules not to carry out his own desires but in order to accomplish God's will for the people. The king is by no means exempt from God's demands; the covenant establishing David on the throne carried with it God's expectation that the king will reign *righteously*. Indeed, the king's real function is to ensure the justice that is the heart of the covenant with Moses. In Psalm 72, the psalmist prays:

> Give the king your justice, O God,
> and your righteousness to a king's son.
> May he judge your people with righteousness,
> and your poor with justice....
> May he defend the cause of the poor of the people;
> give deliverance to the needy
> and crush the oppressor. (Ps. 72:1-2,4)

These verses underline the intimate relationship between God's demand for justice and the king who rules in the name of the God who is Israel's true king. Furthermore, the justice with which the king reigns is defined not by his impartiality, but by his attention to those who need him most. It was a remarkably advanced ideal, and held the promise of a human society in which justice is not only an abstract principle, but also a reality.

But that promise was rarely fulfilled. Human failings and institutional weaknesses conspired with broader circumstances of history to bring Israel to disaster. Civil war, corruption, political and military reversals, and spiritual decay all played a part in reducing the People of God to the condition of a conquered and colonized people.

Through the centuries of disappointment and misery that followed political and military defeat, Israel's covenant with God became a means of maintaining a sense of identity. With the passage of time, the faith of the Jewish people matured and blossomed in the hope that God would continue to be with them. If Israel had once been delivered from slavery, they would be rescued once again.

That hope expressed itself in many ways. It lived on in the dream that some day Israel's life as a people would reflect the reality of their bond with God—a bond created through justice. It was that hope John the Baptist proclaimed by the Jordan River, the same hope that awoke in Jesus when he stepped into its waters. It flourished too in the vivid imagery of the kingdom of God. Jewish sources tell us that the expectation took many forms. We also know, from our own Christian sources, that the same hope and expectation formed the heart of Jesus' message: "The kingdom of God is near at hand!" And we know that Jesus' proclamation of hope was what drew his followers to him and provided their sense of who he was and what he stood for.

Because the reign of God always remained a promise only partially fulfilled for Israel, this image of God's rule gave the first Christians a clear sense of destination—a dream beckoning from the future and making the hard realities of the present far more bearable. We ourselves, as twentieth-century Christians, will never comprehend the passion with which they lived their faith unless we learn something about what they were waiting and praying for. If we can only recover something of that passion and that hope, perhaps we will once again grasp what our ancestors meant when they spoke about "good news."

QUESTIONS FOR REFLECTION

1. How did Israel understand its identity as a nation to be a God-given "calling"? What was its primary mission as a nation?

2. Do you believe this sense of mission has influenced Americans' understanding of their national identity? How?

3. How would a people's belief that God is their ultimate ruler affect their life? Their understanding of their history?

Chapter 3

JESUS AND THE DREAMS OF ISRAEL

---

*C*hained to those in front and behind, the woman struggled desperately to maintain the pace as the prisoners made their way towards the city that waited in the distance. They had been traveling for weeks; the sun was unforgiving, and only the sight of palm trees on the horizon gave her hope that her agony might some day end. Her feet, bloodied and blistered, had lost all feeling. At night, when they were allowed to stretch their exhausted bodies on the ground to gather strength for tomorrow, her dreams plagued her. The siege that had broken the strength of the people of God's holy city, Jerusalem, the shrieks when the Babylonian troops at last entered it and attacked its people with their swords, the unforgettable vision of the Temple in ruins, her last glimpse of Jerusalem as she began the journey towards exile— these memories returned in the night and she awoke, her eyes pouring tears.

There had been five in her family when they set out, bound to the other survivors being driven like animals to Babylon. But the journey had been too much for her husband, and he had died after only a few days into it. His was one of the first of many shallow graves that now lined their route of sorrow. Her daughter lasted for more than a week, but when she stumbled and fell, a soldier quickly ran her body through with a sword. There was no time for mourning; when they reached their destination, she would have more than enough time for grief. And *who would have thought their son, barely seven years old, and her mother, now past sixty, would have survived all the way to their exile in Babylon, never again to see the land they had called home?*

The destruction of Jerusalem and the exile were bitter blows to a people whose life with God had been centered in a Temple that was now destroyed. The God of Israel, who had guided them to the Promised Land, was so bound in their understanding to that holy place they could not imagine that God's presence could reach beyond its boundaries.

The Jewish survivors found themselves far from home; they felt themselves far from God. In that exile, an unknown poet penned what must surely be among the most poignant verses in the Scriptures:

> By the rivers of Babylon—
> there we sat down and there we wept
> when we remembered Zion....
> How could we sing the Lord's song in a strange land?
> (Ps. 137:1,4)

But it was in the milieu of exile and despair that the Jewish prophets of hope began to preach an astonishing message: God had not, after all, abandoned them. To the contrary, God had accompanied them to this strange and unknown place. And not only had God remained at their side, but the same God who rescued them from slavery in Egypt would bring them home again.

Messages of hope for an oppressed and enslaved people are found in many of the prophetic books of the Hebrew scriptures. The concluding chapters of the book of Isaiah provide one of the most memorable visions for imagining what it would

23

be like to live, not in chains but as a people whose lives reflect God's will:

> For I am about to create new heavens and a new earth;
> the former things shall not be remembered
> or come to mind.
> But be glad and rejoice forever in what I am creating;
> for I am about to create Jerusalem as a joy
> and her people as a delight.
> I will rejoice in Jerusalem, and be glad in my people;
> no more shall the sound of weeping be heard in it
> or the cry of distress.
> No more shall there be in it
> an infant that lives but a few days,
> or an old person who does not live out a lifetime....
> They shall build houses and inhabit them;
> they shall plant vineyards and eat their fruit.
> They shall not build and another inhabit;
> they shall not plant and another eat;
> for like the days of a tree shall the days of my
> people be,
> and my chosen shall long enjoy the work of their
> hands.
> They shall not labor in vain,
> or bear children for calamity;
> for they shall be the offspring of the blessed of the
> Lord—
> and their descendants as well.
> Before they call I will answer,
> while they are yet speaking I will hear.
> The wolf and the lamb shall lie down together,
> and the lion shall eat straw like the ox;
> but the serpent—its food shall be dust!
> They shall not hurt or destroy on all my holy mountain,
> says the Lord. (Isa. 65:17-20a,21-25)

Isaiah's vision, written during the Exile, depicts God's city as a setting governed by justice. Work will be purposeful, because all will enjoy the fruits of their own labor. No one will be condemned to spend their days in toil only to have the results taken away for the benefit of another. The presence of God will be constant and intimate, experienced in community. This spiritual and social unity will be reflected in the harmony of the whole creation, expressed in the powerful image of the wolf and the lamb lying down together. All nature is at peace, and "they shall not hurt or destroy in all my holy mountain, says the Lord."

This rich imagery of joy, justice, and peace is complemented by other visions in which the central message is the abundance and plenty with which the earth will be blessed when God's will is fulfilled. All are set in the context of the immediate bond with God that forms the basis of *shalom*. Although we customarily translate this Hebrew word as "peace," the Hebrew conveys not only the negative sense of the absence of violence, but also the positive reality of the blessings that are God's will for the creation, and the result of the covenant between God and the people.

Such messages of comfort and hope sustained the Jewish people throughout their exile in Babylon. But sadly, reality disappointed them.

It is true that there came a time when they were permitted to return to their own lands, to rebuild Jerusalem and worship once again in a temple. But their hopes for building a new Israel, guided by God's demand for justice, went unfulfilled. In spite of the best efforts of teachers and preachers, the promise of a people committed to God's covenant was not met. Things went back to "normal."

Meanwhile, new empires were threatening the region the Jewish people called home. Alexander the Great and his successors effected dramatic changes in the world in which they lived. The Jewish God was ridiculed, Jewish laws and traditions despised or forbidden, Jewish hopes dashed. "Success" as the world knew the term depended upon adapting themselves to the values of their conquerors and accepting their rule. Only a few people held on to the covenant and its promise of justice.

For that faithful remnant, the horizon of their expectations became much wider. As their sufferings increased, so too did their hope. Scholars call the form of faith that sprang up among the faithful of this time *apocalyptic*, because it was based on their belief that their victory over adversity was certain and already clear to those who could see it.

Apocalyptic faith covers a broad range of beliefs, but also has some common elements. In the face of persecution and even death, it assures that God is in charge of destiny and will prevail in the end. It offers little hope for the world as it is, but apocalyptic's faith in the sovereignty of God leads it to affirm God's ultimate victory over the evil that stands in the way of the divine will.

Many of the earlier prophets shared a similar faith. What sets apocalyptic apart is that it conceives of history as "programmed," with little room for change or maneuvering in the light of what is about to happen: God's powerful and imminent intervention to set things right, repaying injustice and faithfulness alike. So apocalyptic faith is fatalistic.

Another novel aspect of this style of faith is its insistence on a clearly-revealed plan for this intervention, known only to the elect—God's chosen few. It is this knowledge of God's plan that gives hope to those who are suffering now. They can endure, certain that their pain will end with God's dramatic judgment, a time of reward for those who remained faithful, and of punishment for those who turned their back on God's demand for justice.

The principal themes of this style of faith can be clearly seen in the Book of Daniel. For the author of Daniel, faithfulness to God makes it impossible to serve other masters, however powerful. Such single-minded loyalty carries with it the threat of great suffering, but God is faithful, and in the end will reward those who have held fast. Apocalyptic offers its believers a key to understanding their sufferings as part of the price of faith, and the hope that will make them worth enduring.

One of the questions about which apocalyptic believers liked to speculate was *how* God's intervention would finally come. Some believed their hope still lay with the restoration of David's heir to the Jewish throne, and the reestablishment of the Jewish kingdom as a "light to the nations." Others, perhaps influenced by religious currents from other peoples, began to speculate about a special, perhaps unique and even heavenly, Servant. The Book of Daniel counts on a human ruler (a "son of man") to bring God's rule; others expected not a human being but *the* human being (the "Son of Man"), God's cosmic deliverer who would rule over a renewed and vindicated people.

But the Hebrew scriptures also preserve another image from the times of oppression and hope: the subject of the four "Servant Songs," brief poetic musings that appear in the work of the prophet of the Exile known as Second Isaiah. Almost certainly these Songs were reflections on Israel's identity as a chosen people, a nation called to God's service.

> Here is my servant, whom I uphold,
> my chosen, in whom my soul delights;
> I have put my Spirit upon him;
> he will bring forth justice to the nations....
> I have given you as a covenant to the people,
> a light to the nations,
> to open the eyes that are blind,
> to bring out the prisoners from the dungeon,
> from the prison those who sit in darkness.
> (Isa. 42:1, 6b-7)

God's servant people is called not for its own benefit but for a special purpose: the mission to be a "light to the nations." Once it has been revealed to them what it means to be bound intimately to God, all the peoples of the earth will long to place themselves in relationship with that God.

Just what is the Servant's message, so powerful that it can serve to draw all people to God? The message is *justice*, the ordering of human life according to God's intentions. But the world is such that justice is not achieved without suffering, and it is in fact God's servant who pays the price.

> I gave my back to those who struck me,
> and my cheeks to those who pulled out the beard;
> I did not hide my face from insult and spitting
> (Isa. 50:6).

The poet even dared believe that a violent and selfish world could be changed by the example of a people willing to suffer for the sake of justice. Might not such an example lead them to amend their ways? Could the suffering of God's people not heal a whole world?

> Surely he has borne our griefs, and carried our sorrows;
> yet we esteemed him stricken, smitten by God,
> and afflicted.
> But he was wounded for our transgressions,
> he was bruised for our iniquities;
> upon him was the chastisement that made us whole,
> and with his stripes we are healed (Isa. 53:4-5, RSV).

The fulfillment of God's will for humankind is so categorically opposed to the ways of the world that nothing less than a servant people prepared to *die* for the earth's people can bring them all together. The undeserved suffering of those who understand and serve God's will makes all the difference, and it is against this new understanding of faith in God that we are to see the plight of the chosen people, led by the Babylonians into exile.

By the time Jesus was born, several centuries after the Exile, the Romans had taken their place in the long procession of military rulers who conquered and dominated his people. Once again, the Jews found themselves longing for deliverance—this time, from the Roman occupation. Once again, they recalled the vision of what their life would be like when God's will came to pass. And once again, they speculated about how and when God would come to save them. The occupation was a bitter burden for the Jewish people. It robbed them of their God-given freedom, compromised their sense of national identity, and worst of all, threatened their ability to live in covenant with God.

But just as God's prophets had once awakened hope among a people in exile, now a preacher clothed in animal skins appeared by the Jordan River. "Repent!" he cried. "Prepare the way of the Lord, make straight in the desert our God's highway." The time has come, when God will visit a people who have been waiting for years and centuries. That coming will bring justice; the earth and its peoples will be tried and shaken, and they will never be the same again. It was this prophet, this preacher of judgment and hope, who walked with Jesus into the river on the day when God's son discovered his identity and his calling.

The deep ruts left by the rain made the road difficult to walk and forced the little group to slow their pace as they made their way south. At times, the breeze carried the salt air from the sea, just a short distance away. From time to time, a break in the trees gave them a glimpse of the beach and the dark blue of the Mediterranean beyond.

29

Here the news about Jesus' healing and teaching had not yet reached the people, so Jesus and his friends had a respite from the crowds. In Galilee, men and women had followed them everywhere. Jesus had become something of a celebrity, as people talked about the amazing things that were happening. It was said that thousands of people had been fed when nothing was on hand but a few loaves of bread and some fish. His friend Simon swore that his mother-in-law had been cured of a fever. A paralytic had walked again. People heard that he had even raised a young girl from the dead—when the period of mourning had already begun. And besides all these stories, there were the astonishing, shocking things they reported that Jesus said.

As they walked along, Jesus turned to his friends and asked them a question. "Who do people say that I am?"

"Well, Jesus," one of them responded, "some people think you are John the Baptist, back from the dead." It was small wonder; when Jesus spoke about God's reign, he sounded very much like the man who had baptized him and who had paid with his life for his outspoken words.

"Oh, yes, and some people think you are Elijah." That too was understandable; many Jewish people believed that Elijah— the prophet who had ridden to heaven in a flaming chariot— would reappear to announce the time when God would come to save Israel.

"Yesterday I heard some people trying to figure out if you were one of the prophets. They said that when you talk about God's love, you remind them of Isaiah, but when you get started on justice, they think of Amos."

Jesus made no reply. He paused for a moment, and then asked another question. "What about you? Who do you say that I am?"

Of course they had been talking about that question for a long time, but never when Jesus was there. There was a moment

*of awkward silence, and then Simon, always impulsive, blurted
out what they had all decided: "You are the Messiah."*

Every one of the books of the New Testament agrees with
Simon Peter's answer. And each of the four gospels tells Jesus'
story as the arrival of the Messiah—the "anointed one"—who is
to accomplish God's will.

Each of these gospels also begins its account of Jesus'
ministry with his baptism by John. Luke pauses to describe in
some detail the *effect* of his baptism on Jesus. At the moment
when he emerged from the Jordan River, Jesus was identified as
God's own beloved son. In the aftermath of that experience he
wrestled with the temptations that such an identity represented.
Alone in the desert, he confronted the possibilities of satisfying
his own personal wants ("Command this stone to become a loaf
of bread") and of using his new power to advance his ambitions
("It will all be yours"). It occurred to him that the Son of God
could draw attention to his own gifts—if he were to throw himself from the pinnacle of the Temple in Jerusalem, would God
not save him? (Luke 4:1-13)

But it was not for this that God's spirit had been poured
out on Jesus as his soaking body rose from the river. Now he
found himself impelled to go home—back to Nazareth, back to
the world where he was known, not as God's Son but as the son
of Joseph the carpenter and Mary his wife.

*The Sabbath found Jesus seated as always with the rest of
the village in the small, plainly-built stone hall that served as
Nazareth's synagogue. He was the reader of the day; standing
before his neighbors, he took the great scroll of the prophet
Isaiah, and found a passage that everyone in the synagogue
knew by heart.*

31

> *The spirit of the Lord is upon me, because he has anointed*
> *me to bring good news to the poor. He has sent me to pro-*
> *claim release to the captives and recovery of sight to the*
> *blind, to let the oppressed go free, to proclaim the year of the*
> *Lord's favor. (Luke 4:18-19)*

That was the only text Jesus needed for what he had to say. He
closed the scroll and handed it to the attendant, who reverently
returned it to its resting place. Every eye was fastened on him;
no one could doubt that something profound, perhaps life-
changing, had happened to him while he had been gone. And
they were right.

"Today," said Jesus,"this scripture has been fulfilled in
your hearing."

Like Mark before him, Luke set out to write about Jesus in terms of the only "good news" worth telling: the arrival of the time for which Israel had been hoping, of which its most creative and visionary leaders had been dreaming. Even John's gospel, which is very different from the other three, identifies a number of Jesus' actions, beginning with the turning of the water into wine at the wedding feast in Cana, as signs. Each of Jesus' "mighty acts" can be interpreted as a sign of the time when God's will is to be fulfilled. These signs and miracles happen bacause Jesus has been anointed with God's spirit.

But of course the last and greatest sign of God's reign is to be found on the other side of Jesus' death: his resurrection from the dead and the gift of God's spirit to his followers. St. Paul understood Jesus' resurrection as the first act of the process by which God's reign reaches its fulfillment. The second act, which still lies in the future, will begin with his triumphant return to initiate God's endless reign, the time foretold by prophets and seers long before. As he wrote to the Christians in Corinth:

Since death came through a human being, the resurrection of
the dead has also come through a human being;... each in
their own order: Christ the first fruits, then at his coming
those who belong to Christ. Then comes the end, when he
hands over the kingdom to God the Father after he has destroyed every ruler and every authority and power (1 Cor.
15:21-24).

But not everyone saw things as Jesus' followers saw them.
Some Jews, who believed firmly that God would one day
deliver them, wondered why nothing had changed for them—if
Jesus was in fact who the Christians claimed he was. Other ob-
jections had to do with the style of Jesus' life and the manner of
his death. There was nothing in the Jewish expectation, either in
or outside the Hebrew scriptures, to prepare people for a Messiah from an obscure Galilean village. Nor were many Jews
comfortable with Jesus' attitude towards the Law, which to
them must have seemed casual and ultimately dangerous.

Most of all, it was Jesus' death that most Jews could not
accept. Their scriptures clearly expressed disdain for death by
crucifixion; it was a shameful way to die. Yet that was precisely
the way in which Jesus met his death. Many of the Jews asked,
how could the followers of Jesus claim that God's Messiah
would be allowed to die such a death? Even the victory of the
resurrection did nothing to take away the shame of his execu-
tion. Yet the Christians were saying that it was precisely
through this shameful cross that God's rule enters human history!

How to make sense of these contradictions, how to respond to these doubts and disagreements? The Christians did
something very natural: they went back to the Jewish scriptures
and began to reread them, this time in the light of what they
knew about Jesus. In their mind, the reign of God that had
formed Israel's hope had now begun; they recalled the promise
of abundance and justice and peace in the light of what Jesus

had said and done: "Today this scripture has been fulfilled in your hearing." In his mighty acts, Jesus was the "Son of Man" named by God to redirect the course of human history. And perhaps most significant of all, in his cross and death he was the Suffering Servant, the "man of sorrows," "acquainted with grief," "wounded for our transgressions." Far from being a sign of God's displeasure, the crucified Jesus is the one with whose stripes we are healed. In Paul's words, the crucified Christ, who is "a stumbling block" and a "foolishness," is for Christians "the power of God and the wisdom of God" (1 Cor. 1:23-24).

Thus the early Christians not only made Israel's hopes their own, but also redefined those hopes and broadened them to include the whole human race. Now the covenant with God and the demand for justice that lies at its heart are no longer limited to the people of Israel. The people of God can now embrace, at least in principle, the whole human family. The Letter to the Ephesians reminds a group of gentiles who have become followers of Jesus that once they were

> aliens from the commonwealth of Israel, and strangers to the covenants of promise, having no hope and without God in the world. But now in Christ Jesus you who once were far off have been brought near in the blood of Christ. For he is our peace; in his flesh he has made both groups into one. (Eph. 2:12-14)

But if the People of God are now bound by a new covenant, the purpose for which they are called has also been broadened. They live with a new understanding of the *purpose* of that holy community. Paul goes far beyond a new vision of the People of God. He (and other Christians of the first century) also adopted as their own Israel's sense of *mission*. Indeed, if Israel was a "light to the nations," they now assigned that role to the newly-defined Christian community.

The gospel writers made a similar point, each in his own way. Luke emphasized this mission at the beginning of his gospel, when he reported how an old man recognized the child Jesus at the time of his presentation in the Temple. Simeon declared that in Jesus he had now seen God's salvation, "a light for revelation to the Gentiles and for glory to your people Israel" (Luke 2:32). Matthew, on the other hand, made precisely the same point in the last verse of his gospel, when the Risen Christ sent out his disciples in what has come to be called "The Great Commission":

> All authority in heaven and on earth has been given to me. Go therefore and make disciples of all nations, baptizing them in the name of the Father and of the Son and of the Holy Spirit, and teaching them to observe all that I have commanded you. Remember I am with you always, to the end of the age (Matt. 28:18-20).

This radically revised image of the People of God, incorporating the Jewish sense of mission but transforming the identity of God's chosen people, shaped the faith of the Christians of the first century and became part of their legacy to future generations. Most Jews could not accept the Christians' reinterpretation of their tradition. Gradually, those who identified Jesus as the messiah found themselves moving farther away from Paul's hope of a community made up of both Jews and gentiles. They still clung, however, to their belief that Christians had inherited God's promises to Israel.

But if Christians were heirs of these promises, they also inherited the dream. God's reign, so long awaited by the people of the covenant, was now eagerly anticipated by a people who saw themselves as the community of a new covenant. The hope remained, broadened and still vivid, to strengthen and animate a people who confidently believed that God was making all things new.

QUESTIONS FOR REFLECTION

1. How did the dreams of Israel influence and shape Jesus' understanding of who he is and what he is for?

2. When Jesus said, "The spirit of the Lord is upon me, because he has anointed me to preach good news to the poor," what do you think those words meant to the people of Nazareth? What do they mean to you?

3. How is his followers' understanding of who Jesus is reflected in their hopes for this world? How does our understanding of Jesus affect what we hope for our world?

Chapter 4

GOD'S CITY, HUMAN CITY

For here we have no lasting city, but we are looking for the city that is to come (Heb. 13:14).

T
he shouts could be heard blocks away. Paul, the rabbi who was now the Christian movement's greatest advocate, had come back to Jerusalem. As always, he tried to walk a careful path between the sensitivity of the Jewish people and his conviction that in Christ, the distinction between Jews and gentiles no longer mattered. He did his best to keep the Jewish law, but when he entered the Temple, the crowds mistakenly took the men with him for gentiles, whose very presence would have been blasphemy in that holy place.

The enraged mob dragged Paul from the Temple, and the massive gate was locked behind them. He would surely have died, but as the blows fell, the sounds reached the headquarters of the Roman army. The crowds fell back as the troops drew near, but they kept shouting for his death.

The religious passions that were frequently unleashed in Jerusalem dismayed the Roman occupying forces, whose only aim was to maintain the peace so that this insignificant corner of the Empire could function efficiently. The tribune in charge, determined to understand the cause of such an unsettling uproar, ordered that Paul be beaten to find out what he would tell them. Such brutal treatment could be given to Romans only if they had been tried and convicted; of course, that safeguard did not apply to the conquered peoples of the Empire.

Paul's bruised and bloodied body was already tied to the post where the beatings were administered. Gasping for breath, he said to the centurion who was about to give the order to proceed, "Is it lawful for you to scourge a Roman citizen who has never been convicted?"

Paul's question changed everything. Soon the centurion's commander appeared. "Are you really a citizen of Rome?" he asked.

"I am," Paul replied.

"It cost me a great deal of money to buy my citizenship," the soldier commented.

"But I," said Paul, "am a Roman citizen by birth."

In the world in which the first Christians made their home, citizenship could literally be a matter of life and death. Citizens of the Empire lived under a system of laws that protected them and gave them access to the institutions of their society. The accident of Paul's birth saved him from a beating and gave him the right to make a personal appeal to the emperor, which brought him eventually to the city of Rome.

Most of the early Christians, however, did not enjoy the rights of Roman citizenship. Life for them was arbitrary, and privileges were few indeed. They were abused and victimized by the occupying power, which stripped them of their property, stole their wealth, ridiculed their faith, and killed them when it chose.

The early followers of Jesus viewed the Empire with passion and contempt because of the contradiction between what they believed God intended for the creation and the world as it existed under Roman rule. It was the Roman authorities who ordered the death of Jesus, while the imperial legions enforced the periodic decrees ordering his followers to burn incense before Caesar's image—an order they frequently refused and for which they were often punished. It was Rome that seemed to be the center of a universe that neither knew nor respected God, but rather appeared to worship itself.

Like their Jewish ancestors in faith, Jesus' followers believed that God had dreamed dreams for the creation and that men and women fulfilled their calling and destiny only when they lived in accordance with those dreams. They understood that to live by God's purposes established a bond of mutual love between themselves and God, a bond of love reflected as well in a human community of perfect justice. Living by the priorities and mandates of God meant accepting God's will as normative for the whole human family. While these early Christian expressed this relationship with God and one another as God's *reign* or *rule*, they did not mean to imply a form of submission to an arbitrary or tyrannical deity. Far from requiring the abdication of human responsibility and freedom, the reign of God called for a maximum commitment to make humanity's values conform to God's.

The prophets insisted that our relationship with God is mirrored in the human society in which we live. Intimacy with God is reflected in plenty, joy, peace, economic justice, and natural harmony. The early Christians explored this idea in the light of their experience with Jesus. Many of his actions were interpreted as signs that God's reign was beginning to make itself visible. But alongside their experience of God's reign here and now, they also assumed its fulfillment would not be long in appearing. Nowhere is that hope expressed more clearly than in the Book of Revelation, the eschatological vision of John of Patmos.

It was not yet dawn. The old man had been writing all night, recording the terrifying visions, the awesome warnings that haunted him at all hours.

Here, at least, there was peace. Patmos, a tiny rock in the midst of the sea, was untouched by the winds of passion and power that rocked the cities of the Roman Empire. Even now, even from this cave to which he had been banished, he could hear the first bird-songs. Later, when the sun had risen, the gentle noise of the sheep on the nearby hillside would keep him company.

He was far from home, but in a sense that had always been true. With his first breath, he had drawn in the dreams of his people, been fed with a sense of God's promises. He knew the contours of God's world-to-come better than he knew the next village. Unlike his parents and their parents, he had had the unimaginable good fortune to live in the light of the One they had been waiting for—Jesus, the Messiah. When he was still young, he had been touched by the preaching of those who had known Jesus, and had become one of them.

Even though he had never seen Jesus, John of Patmos felt as if he knew him—not so much the man who had once walked this earth as John himself walked it, but the glorified Messiah, waiting for the moment when he would return to this proud, faithless earth and make everything new.

John had been waiting, too—waiting, and watching for the signs of his coming. Slowly he had grown old with waiting. There had been moments of high expectation, even times of great joy, when it seemed as if the time were surely right. But there had also been seasons of sorrow, when the Empire had stirred itself, noticed how "these Christians" seemed to be everywhere, and had struck at them cruelly. In those times, the followers of the Way could only wait breathlessly, huddled be-

hind locked doors, rigid with fear when soldiers' footsteps sounded in the street.

John had been fortunate. Was it his age that led the authorities to decree exile rather than death? In any case, this bare and empty island was as good a place to wait as any. And as he waited, the dreams and visions began to come as never before. Rome is a beast seated on seven hills, called "Babylon" in memory of Israel's worst enemy.

> *For all the nations have drunk of the wine of her fornication, and the kings of the earth have committed fornication with her, and the merchants of the earth have grown rich with the power of her luxury. (Rev. 18:3)*

He saw with the eyes of faith the Lamb slain for them, saw the opening of the books where God's plan is written, saw the terrible woes that would fall on those who served the Empire— kings and soldiers and merchants and ship's captains.

And as he saw, he began to write, so that these visions could strengthen others who were also waiting. His mind became a battlefield between Christ and the forces of evil, his soul felt the struggle and the pain. It was as if he were living the anguish of all those Christians who felt the threat of death—and suddenly, he heard their cry: "How long, O Lord, how long?"

John's vision ended with a note of glorious triumph, because he held to the very end his certainty that soon, very soon, it would all be over. What lies on the other side of the persecution is, as Isaiah foretold, "a new heaven and a new earth" (Is. 65:17; Rev. 21:1). But John chose to emphasize the specifically *human* aspect of this recreated earth by focusing on the image of the *city*, the blasphemous city of Rome and the glorious city of God.

> And I saw the holy city, the new Jerusalem, coming down
> out of heaven from God, prepared as a bride adorned for her
> husband; and I heard a loud voice from the throne saying,
> "See, the home of God is with mortals. He will dwell with
> them as their God; they will be his peoples, and God himself
> will be with them; he will wipe away every tear from their
> eyes. Death will be no more, mourning and crying and pain
> will be no more, for the first things have passed away." (Rev.
> 21:2-4)

The description that follows makes it clear that what John
describes is a holy *human community*. A city is by definition an
environment created by human beings; now it has been transformed into a redeemed environment existing in accordance
with God's will. For that reason, the city is a place of abundance and beauty, symbolized by the precious stones and gold
that adorn it; for that reason, too, it is a place of life, where
death and sorrow are forgotten. The source of life is the very
being and presence of God, so intimate and close that there is
no need for a temple. A meeting place is no longer called for;
God's presence is the very environment in which the city lives.
Nor is there any need for the sun; that same presence lights up
the human setting.

But we must not forget that John dreamed his dream at a
time when Christians still feared the possibility of persecution
from the Empire, against which they knew they were powerless.
The experience of Christians in the first years of the church was
a school of suffering, in which they faced not only the ordinary
pain of human experience, but also the special griefs that fell on
them as Christians. We have only to read the New Testament to
understand what sort of world they inhabited.

The world they knew was, above all, a world of *death*. It
is no wonder that the central experience of Jesus' life was his
dying; death was the pervasive reality. In the gospels we meet
its many faces. There is the living death of the lepers, ostracized

from the human community, making their home among the tombs—a pregnant image of their plight. There is the self-righteousness that could stone to death a woman taken in adultery or a young Christian convert named Stephen. There is the premature death of a servant, of a young daughter, of a widow's son. There is the tragic death of a friend, the death-in-life of beggars at the gate. There are the intimations of death, the grotesque and incurable ailments that deformed and pained so many of the characters in the gospels. There is the death of so many of Jesus' friends, executed because they held fast to their faith in his vision. And of course there is *the* death: the cross that casts its shadow over all history.

It is a world of darkness, the image of all kinds of failure to *see*. There are the blind who people the gospels, but also the spiritually blind who miss Jesus' point: the rich young man who cannot give up his wealth, the disciples who fail to grasp the meaning of the signs. There is the darkness that falls over the city as Jesus hangs dying.

The world of the New Testament is also a world of the poor. It is true that the crucial decisions are made by people of affluence and power, but the world through which Jesus and his friends move, and in which they are at home, is a world of stark poverty. We encounter families who provide too little wine for a wedding; fishermen anxious about their catch; a hungry crowd who listen to Jesus with empty stomachs; a woman who rejoices when she finds one lost coin, and another who has only two pennies, which she gives away. We meet a man beaten and left at the side of the road, and a beggar named Lazarus. These poor populate the countryside, the highways, and above all the crooked city streets through which Jesus passes.

And the world of the New Testament is, finally, the world of the city. Jesus is at home among country folk, and draws many of his stories from their life. But the crucial action of the

New Testament takes place in the city, because it is there that humankind lives in the environment it has created for itself, the ultimate human artifact.

The Book of Revelation shows us how those early Christians imagined such a setting after it had been transformed by God's intentions and priorities. But the New Testament portrays a far different urban reality. The city is the setting where Jesus is cheered—and rejected; welcomed—and condemned; presented to God—and crucified. It is the place where God's will is announced—and forgotten. Perhaps the most vivid image of this perspective comes as Jesus approaches Jerusalem:

> Jerusalem, Jerusalem, the city that kills the prophets and stones those that are sent to it! How often have I have desired to gather your children together as a hen gathers her brood under her wings, and you were not willing! (Luke 13:34)

Like the Jews, the early Christians considered the city's failure to stem from idolatry: the worship of false gods. To both groups, the city's insensitivity, corruption, injustice, and violence—in a word, its lack of *humanity*—could be explained only because the city paid homage to other priorities and other gods. And like the prophets of the Hebrew scriptures, the Christians equated idolatry with adultery. If justice and peace issue from a loving relationship with God, then oppression and bloodshed must be the result of turning away from that intimate bond and allying oneself with another kind of power altogether. For the early Christians, the contradiction between this world and the world to come—between the human city and God's city—was absolute and unbridgeable. They could not imagine passing from one to the other without a wrenching cataclysm in which the godless city would be so radically transformed that it would become something altogether different.

But they also understood that the power to make that cataclysmic change lay outside their reach. These believers confidently expected God to intervene and "make all things new"; they hoped it would happen soon, but they knew that the times were out of their control. As Mark recorded in that section of his gospel called the "Little Apocalypse":

> About that day or hour no one knows, neither the angels in heaven, nor the Son, but only the Father. Beware, keep alert; for you do not know when the time will come. (Mark 13:32-33)

Many of the New Testament writings indicate that a mood similar to Mark's apocalyptic pervaded the early Christian community. There was considerable fear and apprehension at the prospect of suffering, but also a sense of watchful expectation, a careful reading of the "signs of the times" in the hope that the City of God would make itself manifest.

In the meantime, what were Christians to do? We know from Paul's epistles that some became idle. They abandoned their daily life altogether and did nothing, depending upon the Christian community to support them. Paul had little patience with them. Reminding them of the rule he had laid down, "Those who will not work, let them not eat," he wrote the Christians in Thessalonica a stern message:

> We hear that some of you are living in idleness, mere busybodies, not doing any work. Now such persons we command and exhort in the Lord Jesus Christ to do their work quietly and to earn their own living (2 Thess. 3:11-12).

Most of the early disciples of Jesus followed Paul's advice and went on working, hoping, and sharing their hope with anyone who would listen.

There was another element to their life, however, that played a critically important part in their experience of waiting. Because they expected the City of God, they considered themselves already in some sense to *belong* to that city. As Paul observed in his letter to the Romans, in their baptism Christians have already been united to Christ in his death and his resurrection. The consequence of that fact is that they no longer belong to this present reality at all; they have already become citizens of God's city. And for Christians, it is the only citizenship that ultimately matters. All other allegiances have become irrelevant. That is why the author of Hebrews remarks that Christians have no permanent city; they are waiting for one that is still to come. Even Paul, who was not above using his Roman citizenship when it served a purpose, ultimately died because he refused to acknowledge Rome's lordship over him.

Such a posture relativizes all attachments to current "cities," all human settings that are rooted in the reality of things as they are. Indeed, the early Christians described themselves as "aliens and exiles" (1 Pet. 2:11).

But—and this is a crucial aspect of their waiting—those Christians experienced signs of God's city already in this world as we live it. The City of God remained a hope for the future, but there were glimpses, "previews," moments in which the reality of that future is already known in the here and now.

The first signs of the City of God were, of course, Christ's resurrection and the pouring out of God's Spirit. But there remains still another, ongoing sign that continues to provide a foretaste of that city: the present experience of the Christian community, the people who "belong" to the City of God. In Paul's words, "If anyone is in Christ, there is a new creation: everything old has passed away; see, everything has become new" (2 Cor. 5:17). The Letter to the Galatians puts it this way:

> As many of you as were baptized into Christ have clothed yourselves with Christ. There is no longer Jew nor Greek, there is no longer slave nor free, there is no longer male or female; for all of you are one in Christ Jesus. (Gal. 3:27-28)

To be baptized—initiated into the Body of Christ—is, then, to belong to a community that neither lives by nor is defined by the present order of things. The usual standards and norms that we customarily use to judge others—the measuring-sticks of religion, social-economic status, and gender—foster inequality, oppression, and injustice. To enter the Christian community is to belong to a new creation, in which all those inequalities have been abolished and transformed. The radical equality held up by Paul for the Christian church is itself a promise and sign of life in the City of God, and issues in the love expressed by the Greek word *agape*.

Although we ordinarily translate *agape* as "love," its meaning in the New Testament is probably nearer to the English word "respect." *Agape* is based neither on emotion nor self-interest; instead, it signifies the obligation we have to respect other human beings, not because they have earned it, but because they are created in God's image. The justice of the City of God—and of the church as its sign—is built upon this recognition of common humanity and common human value. It follows, then, that the life of the church is meant to mirror, not the world as it is, but the world as God wills it to be. The values of God's city—peace, plenty, justice—are to be the values of the Christian community *here and now*.

It goes without saying that the church is both part of and distinct from its human surroundings. While there have always been sectarian Christians who insisted upon rejecting society, the posture adopted by the early church was less one of withdrawal than of awareness of its ultimate allegiance. Many of the New Testament writers attempt, with varying degrees of wisdom, to spell out how to live "in the meantime" between Easter and the final arrival of the City of God. Much of their practical advice is time-bound, reflecting the peculiar concerns and anxieties of the first few centuries after Jesus. But one thing they agree upon is their conviction that Christians do not ultimately "belong" to the world, organized as it is for greed, violence, and injustice. Rather, they belong to God's city. These writers look towards a human community in which justice, plenty, and peace are a reality. They believe that they already have encountered that reality through their life in the Body of Christ. The church is the setting in which they experience, here and now, what God's city is to be, but it is also the community that is waiting for that city to be revealed.

Most of Jesus' earliest followers expected that the wait would not be long. Even when they were forced to endure hardship, they accepted their fate in confidence that soon—very soon—Christ would return in glory and this world would be transformed into the City of God.

They were disappointed.

The Book of Acts tells us that the "mighty acts" that marked Jesus' ministry continued at the hands of his disciples, yet these "signs of the kingdom" remained just that—signs. The fullness of God's reign remained just as distant as it had been when Jesus announced its arrival, while the birth-pangs of the new age seemed to bring nothing new to birth.

From Patmos, John held on to his certainty that the Christ was coming soon, but realized that the delay was weakening the faith and fervor of many: "I have this against you, that you have abandoned the love you had at first" (Rev. 2:4). Others attempted to understand or even explain the delay of the last act of the cosmic drama they were expecting; Paul seems to have comforted himself with the notion that God was giving the world time to repent before Christ returned in judgment and closed off the possibility forever. Still other New Testament writers reinterpreted the notion so that for them the resurrection itself was the "second coming," and God's reign was already here.

Christians influenced by Gnosticism came to terms with the delay by translating their hope into a "spiritual" escape from this material world to the realm of pure spirit. For gnostic Christians, God's reign had nothing to do with transforming the arena of time and history; rather, it is an eternal state of union with God once the soul has been set free from the prison of the body. This last notion was vigorously opposed by the church, which required its members to affirm their belief in "the resurrection of the body" in order to hold on to its hope for the redemption of this world of flesh and blood. The biblical view of human nature rejects the split between *soul* and *body* that pervaded so much of Greek philosophy, insisting instead on the Hebrew belief in the goodness of the created world, including the body. Christians' hope for God's reign assumed that the world itself would share in the transformation that ushers in that rule.

Whatever it chose to believe, the Christian community still had to come to terms with the failure of its immediate expectation that Christ would soon establish God's reign of justice, plenty, and *shalom*.

Less than three centuries after Jesus appeared announcing that God's reign was at hand, the Roman government made Christianity the official religion of the empire and the Emperor Constantine was baptized. Between those historical moments lies a long and often bloody period of confrontation and conversion. Nevertheless, the new perspective brought about by this changed relationship with the imperial power radically altered the way Christians thought and hoped. They no longer anticipated with joy the fall of an empire; instead, they now believed they had converted it. Rome could be the church's ally in mission, and Christians could support and pray for an institution they now understood as God-given, the instrument of God's peace for a troubled and warring humanity.

But the empire that flourished under a Christian ruler was no longer the old Rome. The first Christian emperor moved the capital to the city he named for himself—Constantinople, the "City of Constantine"—while the former center of the world sank into decay. As Christians in the East wrestled with questions of imperial policy, those in the West slid into a long period of invasion, collapse, and submission. Still God's reign was delayed. Still the church recalled those words of Jesus: "The kingdom of God is near at hand."

The history of the church reveals that Christians continued to respond in various ways to the failure of their immediate apocalyptic expectations. Each attempt has tried to do justice to the biblical hope with varying degrees of success, for too much of the New Testament is devoted to that hope for it to be overlooked entirely. As long as Christians read their scriptures and said their creeds, they were reminded, even if dimly, that the end of the story had not yet been told. That hope survived as a legacy to be drawn upon in times of need.

Some Christians maintained the future thrust of their faith by projecting their hopes out of this world and onto heaven. Once the church felt at home in the world of Greek and Roman culture, it began to accept the idea that what mattters about being human is the soul, immortal but imprisoned in a fallible and fallen material world. If this is true, salvation lies not in a *new* world, but in *escape* from the world. God's reign can be pictured as a timeless, heavenly reality, totally unconnected to the world of history. Biblical texts that express negative attitudes toward the world as it is could be interpreted as disdain for the material creation, rather than as a critical prelude to God's new earth. God's reign can be assumed to be unrelated to earthly events, since it is located beyond the world that is our current (and temporary) home.

Countless Christians have shared this otherworldly faith masquerading as Christian hope. Numberless victims of injustice have accepted their fate without ever knowing that God wills for the human family to live in equality and dignity. Generations of the greedy have justified themselves by the reminder that "our citizenship is in heaven," without recalling that such a fact judges every act of inhumanity. This style of faith has pervaded Christian spirituality, led untold numbers of people to make their peace with oppression, and perverted the prophets' vision. Surely the reign that Jesus declared "at hand" is closer than the heaven that remains still beyond our reach.

Nevertheless, the classic apocalyptic hope of the scriptures always reappears—usually during moments of crisis, when the contradiction between daily reality and the biblical vision of hope becomes especially acute. Apocalyptic faith always flourishes in such times of upheaval and contradiction.

One such flourishing occurred at the end of the the Middle Ages and the time of the Protestant Reformation. At that time the radical dislocation of European culture and society spelled the death of the old medieval order, which gave way to a new vision of the world. But many people—especially those on the margins of society—interpreted that time of crisis in the light of New Testament apocalyptic. Because the poor and outcast saw the old world as hopelessly corrupt, they tended to reject any association with the state, judged the "official" churches as compromised, and sought to live according to the values of the new world for which they were waiting. When these dissidents were persecuted—and they were—they read their suffering as the necessary pangs of the new and glorious age to come. In some cases, the more extreme fringe groups even took up arms against the forces of the old order, convinced that in doing so they were hastening the coming of God's reign.

Movements of peasants and the urban poor sporadically shook the face of Europe with armed struggle against the powerful—church, nobles, and merchants. Fueled by their faith that Christ would soon return to establish his reign, convinced that they would be the primary beneficiaries of his justice, the poor saw themselves as God's avengers, punishing the greedy, ridding the earth of their corruptions, and preparing the way of the Lord.

Similar, though less violent, apocalyptic movements have appeared among Christians at other times of cultural and religious crisis. In the nineteenth century, the processes of industrialization and urbanization produced profound dislocations in American society. One of the many religious responses to this rapid change and stress was the reemergence of apocalyptic sects. The Jehovah's Witnesses, for example, appeared first as a group that anticipated Christ's return on a specified date in the 1870s. The survival of this group in spite of repeated postponements is a remarkable phenomenon in American Christianity.

More recently, apocalyptic faith has appeared in response to the terrifying nuclear threats of the last half of the twentieth century. For instance, the Christian fundamentalist author Hal Lindsey has sold millions of copies of his book, *The Late Great Planet Earth* and its sequel, *The 1980's: Countdown to Armageddon.* In both, Lindsey attempts to use the Bible as a key to interpreting current history, in particular the "signs of the times" that he believes predict the imminent return of Christ. Similar messages pervade the preaching of countless sects and even some mainstream churches, as increasing numbers of people find the crises and contradictions of the present beyond their ability to comprehend. Nevertheless, apocalyptic Christianity has tended to flourish best among those most alienated from the institutions and assumptions of their society, and to appear most strongly when victimized people feel themselves threatened by events beyond their control.

Another style of faith that attempts to affirm the reality of Christian hope points in a straight line towards the future. Failing to take seriously the radical rupture the scriptures describe between God's reign and things as they are, this style of faith puts its confidence in progress—the successful human accomplishment of God's purposes. God's reign is a destination that lies at the end of a period of trial-and-error, learning, hard work, and steady progress. God's mighty intervention foreseen in the scriptures disappears, to be replaced by well-directed human effort. In effect, God's purposes are accomplished by those who grasp them and are committed to making them happen.

American culture has been a particularly fertile ground for this kind of faith. The ease with which American history is interpreted in biblical terms has made us particularly open to seeing the future religiously, while our highly-developed work ethic makes us eager to lend a hand to the project. In the nineteenth century, the opening of the West, the freeing of the slaves, and a dizzying succession of technological advances and scientific discoveries led Americans to assume that God's will was finally coming true. A long procession of popular preachers assured the American people that, with faith and hard work, the ancient promises could be realized at long last. The conquest of disease, the dignity and equality of the human family, the elimination of poverty and misery—all seemed to form part of the inevitable outcome of our national history. Its properity must surely reflect God's will, done on earth as in heaven. "Godliness," Episcopal bishop William Lawrence assured his flock as the twentieth century was dawning, "is in league with riches."[4]

It is a long way from Jesus' proclamation that "the reign of God is at hand" to the sidewalk preacher's placard, "Jesus is

Coming Soon." It is equally distant from John of Patmos' visions of an empire's fall to the smug assurance of a baron of industry that his business ventures are carrying God's purposes forward. But whatever forms it has taken through the centuries, the hope proclaimed by Jesus in preaching God's reign survived to illuminate the faith of the church. Far from being restricted to the inner life of the community of faith, its images and expectations have spilled over and shaped the culture in which it takes flesh. No people have been more affected by the dream of the City of God than those who call themselves Americans, and it is to their unique perspective and experience that we now turn.

QUESTIONS FOR REFLECTION

1. The Christians of the first centuries considered that their ultimate loyalty was to God's reign, rather than to any earthly empire or nation. How did that belief affect their faith?

2. How is our world similar to the world of the first Christians? How is it different?

3. How would you compare your attitude towards the government with that of the early followers of Jesus? How do you respond to the text that declares that "here we have no lasting city, but we seek the one which is to come"? (Heb. 13:14)

4. How do you interpret the words of the Nicene Creed that affirm, "He will come again in glory to judge the living and the dead"?

Chapter 5
LOSING OUR WAY

T *he alley runs behind a row of houses that once were home to some of the wealthiest families in the city. But that was long ago; now, they seem to sag under the weight of their occupants. Here a board is missing from the front steps; there, a shutter hangs askew, rhythmically pounding against the wall in the cold, damp wind. Next door, an aged face peers warily from behind a curtain grimy with dust.*

As night falls, a car makes its way slowly down the alley, weaving a path between potholes. Far from the street, it stops; its lights go dark. Soon, figures appear at the alley's entrance, glance over their shoulders, and move into the dusk. They walk quickly, eagerly towards their destination. They assume they will be able to buy what is on their minds; they are not disappointed. In an hour, the car emerges and disappears. Many thousands of dollars have changed hands.

This scene could be set in any city in the United States. The law of supply and demand has never operated more neatly than in the drug traffic remaking the face of American society at the same time it reshapes the world's economy. It is traffic in despair and one of the surest signs that, for many Americans, hope for the future has died.

The themes and images of hope that dominated Americans' sense of themselves survived a number of historical crises and periods of national testing, among them the Civil War. Settlers, leaving behind everything they knew for a homestead they had only heard about, believed they were helping to build a nation with a glorious future. The West beckoned them with its unknown promises. Immigrants flocked to join their lives to the vision, and for a century, ships packed with human beings crammed below their decks poured new blood into the veins of a people thriving on dreams. Politicians not only spelled out the vision, they believed in it.

When success at last made the United States a power to be taken seriously, its people started to think they were, at last, becoming the "city upon a hill" John Winthrop had proclaimed long before. Its young eagerly enlisted to "make the world safe for democracy," secure that if they died, it was in the service of a cause worth dying for. Two bitter world wars did nothing to shake the dream; to the contrary, the sacrifices they entailed fed the commitment to a future that could give life meaning.

The enormous khaki-green plane's belly eased toward the ground, and brief clouds of dust marked where its wheels touched earth. Minutes later, it reached the gate. Inside, a crowd of people waited, tense, straining to see over the heads of those who had pushed to the front. The door opened. Several uniformed figures emerged. And then they appeared, the ones everyone had been waiting for.

The first figure limped down the stairs, grasping the railing; behind him was another, leaning on a cane. Then a pause; the third emerged on crutches, and haltingly began to descend. At the rear of the crowd a woman screamed, "There he is! It's Bill!" The procession slowed; with agonizing hesitation, they emerged one by one, some with grotesque bandages, others missing a leg, or an arm. They lurched into the waiting room, to be met by shrieks, embraces, and tears.

Now they were moving towards the outside world, the world of home and all things familiar, the world they had left for a season, and to which they were returning maimed, crippled, blinded. On the sidewalk another crowd was waiting, mostly young, like the veterans themselves, with banners and signs: "Give Peace a Chance," "US Out of Vietnam Now." As they surged from the airport, the shouting began: "Criminals!" "Butchers!" "Murderers!"

Robert Bellah's book, *The Broken Covenant*, gave a name and amassed the evidence for a truth we all know. The vision of the covenant community, which held Americans together as a people and pointed them towards the future, has been fragmented. The beliefs, dreams, and expectations we once shared have become, in Bellah's words, "an empty and broken shell."[5]

The rupture of the covenant has been clear for several decades. The civil rights movement and its aftermath demonstrated that many Americans had no share in shaping their community. For centuries, the American people had used a set of biblical images to provide a common national destiny. The crisis of the 1960s proved that many Americans had been denied their place within its framework.

But the reality of racism and discrimination proved to be only the tip of a social and cultural iceberg. Before the United States had seriously addressed its inequalities, it found itself engaged in a war that further divided the national consensus. Opposition to the Vietnam War and its aftermath pitted generation against generation, revealed deep rifts between social classes and geographical areas, and sharpened the consciousness of the two Americas—black and white. Significant numbers of Americans burned their country's flag, refused to register for military service, fled abroad to avoid fighting in the war, and adopted fashion styles designed to show their militant disagreement with their country's policy. The civil religion of the United States was shown to be a veneer covering over deep divisions. Rituals that used to bind people together—the Pledge of Allegiance to the flag, patriotic holidays like the Fourth of July—were often ridiculed or ignored.

As we ponder the collapse of the covenant that bound Americans together as a people, we are confronting what is a religious crisis on a national scale. "Civil religion," which interpreted our identity in biblical terms, has lost its power. One question cries out for an answer: What happened? If a common dream has been broken, it is not enough to take note of that fact. We must ask ourselves who, or what, killed the dream.

In the scriptures, the image of the City of God stands over against the world, judging the way things are and offering an alternative vision of human possibility. Indeed, it is precisely the *difference* between the world as it is and what it might be that provides the basis of hope. But America's religious self-understanding removed the distance and the difference between its own reality and the reality of God's city. The City of God is not ultimately different from the American experience of itself; it is only further down the road, America with the wrinkles ironed out.

The "American dream" reached its zenith as the new television medium enchanted the nation in the period following the Second World War. The prosperity and the opportunities that followed the war opened new horizons for many Americans. Through programming and advertisements, television celebrated an image of American destiny: the family in the suburbs, enjoying the material blessings that follow from living as they are supposed to live.

Life in the sitcoms of the 1950s was funny and fun. Homes were well tended and filling up with new "labor-saving" devices. Cars were long, sleek, and easy to drive on the system of interstate highways just beginning to be built. Families were stable, united, and the only unit of society that really mattered; all other relationships were peripheral and merely fleeting. It would appear that the vision of the Book of Revelation had come to pass. A whole generation of television families seemed to be at home in the City of God: "He will wipe every tear from their eyes. Death will be no more; mourning and crying and pain will be no more, for the first things have passed away" (Rev. 21:4).

In this imaginary world that was beamed via the TV set to millions of American homes, there was no unemployment or economic hardship. There was no divorce, no demonic obsessions like alcoholism or drug addiction, no rebellion by children against their parents. Suffering was reduced to temporary inconveniences and misunderstandings that could be put right in the requisite twenty-eight-minute time frame. Cancer, car accidents, and death itself were banished. Surely this vision of the suburbs was derived from the biblical image of the City of God. Indeed, so fully had Americans achieved their promise that the one "ordinary" activity missing from sitcom society was church-going—as if, like the City of God in John's vision, suburban America no longer had need for a Temple.

The problem, of course, is that it was not true. The image of the "good life" held by the entertainment media may have given many people a vision of what they ought to hope for, but it was only a fantasy. It overlooked altogether the negative side of American society, the many ways in which it failed to measure up to the dreams of God's city. Black Christians and others who failed to share in the "American dream" knew of the distance between what they lived daily and the promise of the

City of God. The churches that lived squarely in the mainstream of white America, however, did not understand that distance, but tended to accept only the suppositions of their culture.

During the decade of the 1950s, large numbers of American churches moved their congregations to the suburbs. They abandoned the inner city, erected large and expensive places of worship in order to "fit in" with their surroundings, and embraced, as their primary task, the labor of helping people conform to this vision of prosperity and happiness. In many ways, the churches participated in the denial of the unpleasant realities—the faces of death—that lurked around them. The churches of the white mainstream provided almost no leadership in looking realistically at their world. If they had, they would have seen the inequalities, the pain, the want, the tragic legacy of slavery and discrimination, the millions of Americans who struggled to survive, the broken families and lost children. But they did not.

As late as the 1960s many, perhaps most, Americans still assumed that a God-given mission was an important part of their national identity. In that decade, two very different efforts were launched by the United States on the grounds that it had an obligation to act on behalf of other nations. The first, initiated by John F. Kennedy, was the Peace Corps. Presented as an opportunity for Americans, especially the young, to share the benefits of their "good life" with poor peoples, a small army of well-intentioned volunteers was sent to many of the least developed areas of the world. A few years later, President Lyndon Johnson committed American military assistance to the Republic of South Vietnam in order, he said, to prevent its fall to its Communist neighbors to the north.

Each of these efforts drew upon the time-honored sense of mission that had led Americans to wish to share their ways with others. Each demonstrated the native sense of superiority that had been instilled in the way Americans viewed their way of life. Each, in its own way, was a failure.

It is true the Peace Corps accomplished countless concrete successes: schools built and staffed, wells dug, agricultural projects planned and executed. But the underlying purpose of the Peace Corps was far deeper. It was based on a policy that saw American-style democracy as right and appropriate for all peoples. The Peace Corps was one arm by which the prosperity necessary for democracy could be prepared.

That hope failed. In country after country, the efforts of the Peace Corps foundered on the hard facts of poverty. Many came to understand that such poverty was not necessarily accidental, but the side effect of policies freely chosen in order to enrich individuals and groups who profited from the way things were. The hope of the 1960s, which saw American-style democracy as the wave of the future, fell before a wave of military coups and right-wing dictatorships on the one hand, and popular Marxist movements on the other.

The story of American involvement in Vietnam is equally the story of failure. Not only did the United States fail to reach its goal of preventing a communist victory, but its efforts were also undertaken with methods that destroyed an entire nation, left large tracts of land untillable for generations, and created chaos in American society. The Vietnam War proved, for those willing to learn, that the United States had no special mandate to export its culture to those who had not requested it and for whom it was alien and destructive.

The failure of the Peace Corps and the experience of the Vietnam War did not stop American involvement in the affairs of other nations. But its rhetoric has changed. Only occasionally is such activity now justified on the grounds of "doing for" another people. Rather, it is clearly motivated by American self-interest, which is its own justification. The enormous role the

United States has played in Central American in the 1980s and 1990s, for example, does not depend on a sense of mission; it is explained as a necessary action in order to protect American borders and the American way of life.

The scriptural model of the City of God provides us with criteria for evaluating any human society. The root value it proposes is *justice*, which issues in peace and plenty, harmony with God and with nature. All rest upon a conception of what it means to be created in the image of God. Individuals are worthy of living in God's city, not because they have earned it, but because God has created them to be its citizens. The dignity due human beings is, then, inherent in the very nature of being human.

This concept measures the quality of the *community*. Justice always becomes concrete in the relationships that exist among specific persons—husband and wife, parent and child, tenant and landlord, employer and worker. But those relationships are not private but public; they invariably occur within the framework of society and have their effect upon it. The whole community is involved in every abuse of human dignity, and this idea of solidarity is one of the great insights of the biblical tradition.

How does contemporary American institutional life measure up to the biblical imagery of the reign of God?

No more shall there be in it an infant that lives but a few days, or an old person who does not live out a lifetime (Isa. 65:20). In his vision of the reign of God, the prophet Isaiah cited the young and the elderly as two groups whose fate indicates whether God's reign has been fulfilled—no doubt, because he knew well that children and the aged are often unable to plead their own case and are therefore dependent on others for their well-being.

+In spite of an average per capita income that makes the United States one of the richest countries in the world, its rate of infant mortality ranks *twenty-second* among the industrialized countries.

+Both destitution and the sense of being forgotten or tossed aside degrade the elderly poor, often radically shorten their lives, and create nearly overwhelming obstacles to enjoying the "fullness of life" that is theirs by right.

+A debilitating illness can easily exhaust resources long before death comes. Current policy dictates that community assistance is available only when the elderly have spent whatever they possess. They may well find it necessary to sell their home and declare themselves indigent before society comes to their aid.

+Another challenge is the specter of living and dying unnoticed in a nursing home. These peculiarly American institutions, grim witness to our geographical mobility and the fragility of family ties, are often the last stopping place before death. Most are places of loneliness, despair, and abandonment.

They shall not build and another inhabit; they shall not plant and another eat.... they shall not labor in vain, or bear children for calamity (Isa. 65:22-23). Isaiah thought that when God's will is done on earth as in heaven, workers will no longer be exploited for profit, or forced to toil at meaningless jobs in sub-human conditions.

+Millions of jobs have been lost to American wage earners because corporations have found it more profitable to rely on workers in other parts of the world where wages are lower, safety requirements less rigorous, and employees more passive and easily controlled than in the United States.

+The widening gap between rich and poor Americans reflects the disappearance of many jobs that formerly paid wages at a middle-class scale. While new jobs continue to be created, a larger percentage are at the earning level of the minimum wage. Columnist Tom Wicker wrote in 1987:

> A cause for long-term economic and political concern is the "down-scaling" of the U.S. labor force and the consequent decline in the American standard of living. That's because most new jobs being created are in the service sector and tend to pay lower wages and provide fewer benefits; and because many workers displaced from high-wage manufacturing jobs are being re-employed in such lower-paying service jobs.

Citing a study made in the mid-1980s by the Department of Labor, he noted that the shift in jobs had fallen most heavily on minorities; in a five-year period, only 42% of blacks and 52% of Hispanics who had lost their jobs were reemployed.

> If those entering the work force also are finding themselves in demand mostly for low-paying, low-skilled jobs—in many cases they are also temporary or part-time—the real bad news is for society as a whole; a declining standard of living for the working and middle classes; fewer or weaker benefits such as health insurance and pensions; ... more working wives hence more "latch-key children."[6]

+Those unlucky enough to be without work must fend for themselves. In cities across America, families survive in so-called "welfare hotels" where they share their homes with prostitutes, addicts, and drug pushers. In such settings, children often turn to street crime in order to augment their family's chances of survival. If they happen to go to school, they are ostracized by children who enjoy a different standard of living.

+The same process forces the unemployed onto the streets, where they must choose between crowded, drug-infested shelters and doorways. We may meet them begging in subways, on street corners, or in railway stations. They spend hours waiting for food in overtaxed community kitchens dependent on private charity for their survival.

+By the late 1980s, despair was sweeping the American farm community, as thousands of families lost their property. In Oklahoma alone, in a two-year period, one hundred farmers committed suicide. Commenting on this tragic aspect of the growers' "long march of hardship," one journalist observed that for some farmers the frustration and pain that results where the work of generations is undone in a season or two is too much to live with.

+Banks and corporations, in the United States and other developed nations, have contrived to keep most of the world dependent on their capital. Governments in the poor countries have been forced to borrow massive amounts at interest rates that sap their nation's income. Products grown or produced in these dependent economies—sugar, agricultural products, raw materials—sell at prices often below those of twenty years ago. Finished manufactured goods, on the other hand, are marketed zealously and sold in poor countries at vastly inflated prices. This relationship of dependence, fostered by an international debt that has resisted all efforts to control it, guarantees that the wealthy nations will have a source of cheap materials and ready-made markets for their products, but at the price of widespread misery throughout the rest of the world.

The wolf and the lamb shall feed together, the lion shall eat straw like the ox (Isa. 65:25a).

In Isaiah's vision of a creation at peace with God, the discord that plagues the natural order has been overcome and the whole of nature is at one with itself and its creator.

+Acid rain from uncontrolled American industries falls on fields hundreds of miles from its source, poisoning the water and passing into the food chain, to affect human and animal life years later.

+Agribusinesses frequently fail to instruct their workers in proper safety precautions, so that many run advanced risk of disease and death through contact with pesticides.

+The irresponsible disposal of waste has ruined rivers, threatened water supplies, damaged farmland. Nuclear waste, which remains hazardous for thousands of years, litters the countryside and is regularly transported through residential areas by truck and train.

+The keystone of the American system of military defense is the atomic arsenal which, if used, might well eliminate all life from our planet.

+Pollution of the atmosphere from countless sources risks destroying the ozone layer that protects the earth from the sun; the resulting "greenhouse effect" could be disastrous. Scientists warn that the melting of the polar ice cap could inundate coastal cities around the world, while exposure to unfiltered ultra-violet rays increases enormously the possibility of cancer. Changes in the earth's climate would also radically affect the possibility of food production adequate to the world's needs.

They shall not hurt or destroy on all my holy mountain, says the Lord (Isa. 65:25b).

Perhaps no text sums up more succinctly the meaning of *shalom* than Isaiah's vision of God's holy mountain, unmarred by violence. It is a vision that clashes sharply with the reality of American life in the last decade of the twentieth century.

+Expenditures for military purposes stagger the imagination. Even when planners admit that no nation on earth poses a significant threat to the security of the United States and the "cold war" is declared to be over, the military budget consumes a major portion of our country's income, draining resources from education, health care, housing, transportation, and community services.

+American military aid supports repressive dictatorships in many parts of the world, because it is believed they will cooperate in defending American "interests." These regimes often depend on terror and torture to remain in power.

The ultimate biblical criterion for evaluating the quality of justice is the way a society treats those who cannot defend themselves: the weak, the poor, the young, and the old. We must ask ourselves how our society behaves towards those least able to care for themselves: the mentally ill, the physically disabled, those whose family responsibilities overwhelm them, the illiterate and the under-educated, the chemically-dependent and addicted, and the unemployed. Insofar as these people must fend for themselves, without the care or interest of the society of which they are part, we must confront the reality of the land in which we live; it is a far distance to the vision of God's reign we once meant to serve.

"Mommy, I miss Daddy. Why doesn't he come home and live with us like he used to?"

"Darling, you know we've already talked about that. Daddy isn't going to come home and live with us. Daddy has another place to live."

As usual when this topic of conversation came up, Nancy's eyes filled with tears. "Doesn't Daddy love us any more?"

Her mother's voice was tense, pained. "Sweetheart, you know Daddy loves you. He came to see you last Saturday, and this weekend you're going to spend two whole days with him in his new apartment."

"But if he loves me, why did he move away?"

"Nancy, I know this is hard for you to understand, but you have to try. Daddy loves you, but there are some things he

*wants to do with his life that he can only do if he lives by him-
self."*

"What things, Mommy?"

*"Well, Nancy, you know that when Daddy lived here, he
had to spend most of his time taking care of things we all
needed. Remember how he spent every Saturday working
around the house, mowing the lawn, going shopping? Well,
Daddy felt that as long as he lived here, he would never have
time to do any of the things he wanted to do. It makes me very
sad, but I understand what he meant, and you have to try too."*

*"But, Mommy, there are lots of things I want to do, and
you tell me I can't. How come Daddy gets to do whatever he
wants?"*

American culture has always prided itself on the high pri-
ority it places on the individual. Individual rights are at the core
of the founding documents of this nation. The circumstances of
its settlement—the ruggedness of the frontier, the empty spaces
of the West, the natural dangers—rewarded the development of
strong individuals and ensured that those virtues would be at
the heart of the national character. Ralph Waldo Emerson's
essay extolling the theme, while written early in the nineteenth
century, is still being read with reverence in public schools at
the end of the twentieth.

But strong as that individualism was, its fulfillment was
always understood to lie in the community formed by commitment to the covenant. Individualism without the bonds and con-
straints of a sense of participation in community is a new
phenomenon. Its immediate effect on the American family has
been a rapid change in attitudes toward marriage and divorce.
The focal point of marriage is no longer its status as a social
unit, or even the care of children. Instead, it is widely believed

to exist solely for the benefit of each partner, who are free to dissolve it at will if they feel the marriage no longer meets their wishes or needs. Parenthood is similarly defined as a matter of individual choice, either by the parents, or—ultimately—by the wishes of the mother.

The decline of commitment to any community leads people to consider goal-setting as a private project. Education has accordingly been redefined, not by social criteria, but by how well it provides the tools believed to aid in individual progress and mobility. The last decade has witnessed the emergence of specialized private education that proposes to aid children's chances of access to prestigious schools and colleges—considered necessary if they are to survive in a world defined as "everyone for themselves." The appearance of the so-called "yuppies" is directly related to the new individualism. As the group becomes an ever more powerful force in American culture, it has effects on housing, urban planning, transportation, marketing, child rearing, education, and fashion.

Meanwhile, government policy has eagerly endorsed this new personal style. Just as American culture formerly tempered individualism with a strong sense of community, the role of government in protecting personal rights coexisted with responsibility for the well-being of society. That is why the twentieth century gave birth to so many government social programs to improve the quality of community life: Social Security and Medicare for older Americans, the G.I. Bill for veterans of its wars, and a host of other programs that culminated in the "War on Poverty" during Johnson's presidency.

The process of several decades by which government had undertaken to improve the fabric of American life came to an end in the 1980s. A series of counter-moves reversed many earlier initiatives as government, embracing the ideology of individualism, abandoned its responsibility to care for society.

Children, the elderly, the handicapped, young people of college age, the "working poor," all felt the effects of this withdrawal.

Its effect, furthermore, is greater than the sum of each individual budget cut, since it represents a fundamental shift in policy. Government no longer is seen as the appropriate agency in caring for the health of the society as a whole. Individuals are expected to "do for themselves" or rely on the charity and good intentions of their neighbors. The signs are all around us. Homeless people who once lived in subsidized housing now sleep in the streets; thousands of the mentally ill, formerly housed in state hospitals, wander aimlessly; the children of the poor are forced to leave college because neither aid nor loans are available for tuition; and even middle-class families in the same situation incur debts that cripple them for years. This is the portrait of a society made up of autonomous and unrelated individuals when the bond of community has weakened and virtually disappeared.

The consequences for personal ethics appear clearly in an analysis of American teenagers' attitudes towards business ethics, presented by Dean Herbert London of New York University. "Seemingly," he writes,

> today's television heroes—and heroines—whose immoral behavior is sumptuously rewarded have become role models for many young Americans. Moreover, there appeared to be consensus that if you can get away with certain actions ... that translate into wealth, status and power, then the stigma of immorality is mitigated by rewards. ... What is troubling is that the bounds of appropriate behavior have been stretched to incorporate deceit, adultery, blackmail—behavior frequently condoned on television.[7]

What are we to make of these observations? They are vignettes of current reality, part of the truth about us as a people. They provide a way for American Christians to examine their national life in the light of the City of God, and to confront the many ways in which justice as the Bible describes it is missing from that life.

The decline not only of justice, but also of *concern* for justice that American culture has suffered, happened primarily because its individualism has been allowed to flourish without an appropriate attention to community and to the covenant that creates it.

What is ultimately at stake is the model of the "good life" we embrace as a people. What do we hope for? What do we work for? Our culture has offered us unbridled consumerism, in which the good life is measured by tangible possessions that function as emblems of status. Although these vary depending on where we locate ourselves within society, they still function in the same way. Clothing, cars, housing, even pets and vacations, can tell us we have "made it"—that we are living the good life.

The same culture that applauds the piling up of possessions also encourages the individual's amassing of "experiences." These can give a similar sense of status, particularly if they are also costly. Contemporary American fiction, theater, and film is peopled with characters who careen from one experience to the next, looking for ever greater thrills and new titillation in the hope they will achieve, at least for a moment, the "good life." They provide the model for countless Americans who find themselves seeking ever wider promiscuity, ever more potent drugs, and expanding sources of money to continue their search. Such a way of life can exist only when the individual has been totally divorced from a community of meaning and caring. Consider these excerpts from a recent novel about affluent teenagers in Los Angeles, written when its author was still in his teens:

> *"What do you care about? What makes you happy?"*
> *"Nothing. Nothing makes me happy. I like nothing," I tell her.*

> *"Did you ever care about me, Clay?"*
> *I don't say anything, look back at the menu.*
> *"Did you ever care about me?" she asks again.*
> *"I don't want to care. If I care about things, it'll just be worse, it'll just be another thing to worry about. It's less painful if I don't care."*
> *"I cared about you for a little while."*
> *I don't say anything.*

> *...The images I had were of people being driven mad by living in the city. Images of parents who were so hungry and unfulfilled that they ate their own children. Images of people, teenagers my own age, looking up from the asphalt and being blinded by the sun.*[8]

It's a long way to the City of God.

The currents and tendencies that have changed the nation's sense of itself have also affected American Christianity. Because of their past, black Christians and, to some extent, Roman Catholics have retained a faith that takes public realities seriously. But the churches of middle-class America have been caught up in the *privatization* of Christian faith. Overemphasis on personal experience, conversion, and response gradually weakened their resolve to involve themselves in questions of social, political, or economic importance. Those arenas were largely left to civil religion, which was supposed to be based on biblical values and could therefore coexist with a more personal and private faith acted out in the churches. White Protestantism by and large has abandoned the public sphere and committed itself to caring for the personal "spiritual" needs of its constituency.[9]

Many American churches have, therefore, become voluntary associations sought out by those with needs—for companionship, nurture, meaning—that they identify as "spiritual" in nature. However, the suppositions of both the institutions and their members preclude asking a hard question: *Why* must

Americans go searching for dimensions of human experience that most societies have taken as givens? It would appear that limiting faith to the personal and "spiritual" has in fact truncated that wholeness of life of which the Bible speaks. Not only have we learned to define faith in terms of the personal and internal needs of each believer, but the *practice* of that faith also has often been confined to the same realm. The churches' current interest in spiritual direction can be interpreted as a symptom of faith forced into the narrow confines of the private and personal.

Even when the Christian community grasps the social dimension of its calling, it often limits its efforts to gestures that fail to challenge the prevailing realities. We can surely applaud the sometimes heroic means used by some Christians to meet the needs of the hungry and homeless; indeed, in recent years religious institutions have borne the brunt of that burden. But we might also ask if those who undertake such actions are equally concerned to examine and eliminate the *causes* of American poverty, or if they are content merely to bind the wounds without eliminating their source. The American churches' willingness to embrace the spirit of volunteerism called for by current government policy reduces care to individual (and private) choices and good intentions. The danger is that their action accepts and supports yet another erosion of the sense of community that holds a people together. It is good to respond to human need with gestures of caring, but the demand of justice is not satisfied by feeding the hungry; it calls for a world in which there is no hunger. God's justice has not been achieved when a church opens its doors to the homeless, but when a nation assures all its people a decent place to call home.

Unfortunately, the commitment to such a dream seems far from the consciousness of the American people, even the Christians among them. American Christianity has abandoned its sense of future hope. If it speaks of the future at all, it is only to reinforce belief in an afterlife for individuals when they die. This is nowhere more evident than in the churches' role in American funeral practices. Their ministry at the time of death focuses almost uniformly on assuring mourners of the personal survival of the departed. There is almost never mention of the much broader aspect of *resurrection* that looks forward to a new creation. Just as most Americans no longer expect the world to be any different than it is now, so most American Christians suppose that what they hope for lies, if anywhere, on the other side of death. The richness of the biblical vision has been reduced to a question of personal survival: witness our continuing fascination with books such as Elizabeth Kuebler-Ross's *On Death and Dying* and *Life After Life*.

Because hope for the future is the starting point for Christian faith, its loss must distort and weaken the whole of faith. Because that hope has an earthly dimension, spiritualizing it makes it a faith Jesus never taught or knew. Since that hope envisions the future of a people, a faith that is only personal can never embrace what Jesus proclaimed and awaited. American Christianity has been disfigured by its failure to hold on to the fulness of its faith. All of us suffer the consequences.

QUESTIONS FOR REFLECTION

1. How do you respond to the author's assertion that "the vision of the covenant community, which held Americans together as a people and pointed them towards the future, has been fragmented"? What do you consider the most serious effects of that "broken covenant"?

2. What are the positive aspects of individualism? What are its limitations?

3. How does current American culture define "the good life"? How does this vision differ from that of the City of God?

4. How do American churches keep alive the vision of God's city? How do they fail? Do you agree with the author that "American Christianity has abandoned its sense of future hope"?

Chapter 6
ALREADY BUT NOT YET

*T*he sound began as a rumble, a constant thunder, beyond the horizon. As it grew louder, dogs began to growl and bark nervously. Men and women started from their beds and hammocks, children stirred in their sleep. And then it began: like perverse lightning, streaks of light plummeted towards the earth, each followed by a deafening explosion. The Rodriguez's house was consumed by flames. The donkey tethered nearby shrieked with terror. Tito, their youngest child, lay motionless in the path; his mother screamed uncontrollably as her husband held her back from trying to reach him. Everywhere there were cries of pain, of horror, of grief. At the far end of the village, old Senor Porfirio knelt helplessly. In the light of the flames his wife lay dying, blood streaming from her mouth.

The bombing seemed to go on forever, but at last the sound of the engines grew dim, the planes disappeared, and the survivors looked about them as dawn broke. The screams had subsided, and only moans and muffled crying broke the silence. Of the eleven houses that made up the village, three had been destroyed completely. None had escaped without damage. A pile of stones remained where the church's tower had stood. Only a year before, the people of the village had held raffles, saved precious coins, and offered their own labor to erect the tower; now it was gone, destroyed in a few moments by unseen figures who shrugged at the misery they had rained from the heavens.

The ruins of their home were still smoldering when the Rodriguez family brought the broken body of their seven-year-old son and placed it before the church's altar. Minutes later, neighbors bore the remains of Dona Alicia, Senor Porfirio's wife, to a resting place at the child's side. The survivors gathered quietly; they filled the tiny chapel.

Manuela Rodriguez, her child's body before her, stood before the anguished congregation. Her voice trembling, she began to speak.

"Brothers and sisters!" she began. She paused to find the words, and went on. "We are together in our grief. We all know why this has happened to us. It was my own brother who helped us form the cooperative, to try to work together instead of going our separate ways. And we know how much hope he gave us, and how we believed him when he told us that we must struggle to find a better life. We all know the cost of such a struggle. That cost has come home to us. My son lies dead before our eyes.

"Perhaps now you expect me to tell you that we made a mistake. Perhaps you expect me to blame my brother for teaching us how to work together. But I say to you, in spite of what they have done to me and my family, I will not give up our struggle. God is with us. God wills for us to live with justice. God does not decree our misery, our poverty, our pain. We know God longs for us to build a new future, a better future. God promises us a different world than what we have always known.

"We know who has done this to us. It is the few who have denied us what we need to live decently, who have stolen our work from us, who have tried to keep us frightened and powerless. But we know that God is with us when we stand up for justice and so, today, I pledge myself to carry on with our dream. They have killed my son. But they have not taken away my faith,

they have not taken away my hope, they have not taken away my God. "

Julio, one of the few people in the church who could read, stood up. "Listen to what I have found in Matthew's gospel!" he exclaimed, and began to read the story of Jesus' birth. When he came to the verses that described the massacre of the children of Bethlehem, a murmur spread among the congregation.

"Just think!" said Julio. "When God sent Jesus to be born into this world, they tried to kill him too! Think how many families in Bethlehem felt what we are feeling! They knew what it was like to lose their relatives, just because some people hated everything Jesus stood for. But Mary and Joseph stood firm. They did their best to protect Jesus, so that he would grow up to offer his life for the people who needed him. "

He began to sing softly; amid the sobs and groans, the music swelled. Like Christians all over Latin America, they knew the words by heart: "Cuando el pobre cree en el pobre, ya podremos cantar libertad ... When the poor believe in the poor, then we will be able to sing about freedom. "

If Christians in North American have lost their way towards the City of God, they need guides who will help them rediscover their destination. In other parts of the world, Christians have grasped the power and the promise of God's city as an image of earthly hope. They have found their faith and their life transformed as they have oriented themselves towards God's promises. Perhaps their journey can be of help to American Christians as we seek to find our way.

The rediscovery of the City of God as a vivid image for faith has taken place in many parts of the world, but it is the Latin American church that has explored its meaning most fully. Indeed, that rebirth has changed the face of Christianity and blossomed in a movement that could have profound consequences for Christians around the world. Although it began in the Roman Catholic Church, it is not limited to it, but has had effects in other communions as well.

The City of God (which most Latin American theologians prefer to call by the New Testament phrase, *kingdom of God*), was rediscovered when Latin American Christians began to read the Bible for themselves. At the Second Vatican Council, the Roman Catholic Church attempted to make itself more at home in the modern world. It called for its members to act out their faith in the concrete setting in which they found themselves. The church's worship was translated into the language of the people, local music and art incorporated into the liturgy, and the church's membership encouraged to take a more active role in the life of both church and community. One early effect of this reform was that Roman Catholic laypeople began reading and studying the Bible for the first time.

The customary setting for this new awakening is the "base community." These are small groups of Christians, mostly poor, who meet together regularly to study the Bible in the light of their own lives, to pray, and to reflect upon that daily reality. They are sometimes joined by priests or nuns, some of whom may even exercise a leadership role in the base community. However, the focus of the community is the experience and reflection of the *people*, not the leaders.

At the same time, a number of trained theologians have allied themselves with this movement of renewal and attempted to spell out in a systematic way the perspective that is emerging from the base communities. They call their efforts "liberation theology," because its foundation is people's experience of their struggle to be free.

The base communities came into being in order to look at all of life in the light of the gospel. As people examined the reality of their world, they realized that the fundamental truth—before which all else fades into insignificance—is the crushing lack of freedom they experience. Latin America is a continent in bondage. Poverty, illiteracy, exhausted farmland, and cities that can never provide work for all their people guarantee that the overwhelming majority are locked into a situation from which there is no escape. The struggle to survive is the primary struggle.

These are not new truths; they have been part of the reality of Latin America since colonial days. But in recent years, Christians have begun to ask *why*.

For centuries, the Christian churches assured the masses that they were poor because it was God's inscrutable will for this sinful earth. Salvation would come to them if they remained faithful, obeyed the teachings of the church and those who held authority over them, and accepted the way things are as part of God's design. If this earth is a vale of tears, the merits of the Virgin and the saints would carry them to a better place when they die. A whole piety evolved to provide the comfort and support necessary for making their way through the long sorrow that is human existence. The broken Christ of Good Friday seemed to symbolize the human condition; Latin America's poor embraced him as their own.

The impulse of the Vatican Council towards understanding and embracing the world meant that these old attitudes were no longer acceptable. If most people were suffering from poverty and hunger, then there had to be reasons—concrete reasons rooted in the world—for their misery. As Christians set out to learn the reasons for their hardship, they became aware that other forces were indeed at work in shaping their reality. They discovered that the institutions of their society—the structures through which power and privilege were exercised—in fact were designed to provide benefits for the very few.

In some countries it was found that much of the land belonged to a handful of families (in El Salvador, for example, *los catorce*—the fourteen). For generations they had dominated the economic life of a whole people. In other countries, a single family could grasp power and manipulate the national life in ways that brought it almost inestimable wealth. The Somoza family of Nicaragua held land, controlled industries, and stole the money raised around the world for relief when the city of Managua was struck by an earthquake.

But even in large countries beyond the control of a single family and group, the number of people with access to power was tiny. The armed forces customarily supported their power. The rulers alone determined the jobs to be handed out and the land to be leased. Services taken for granted in the developed countries—medical care, access to schooling—were almost unknown among the poor of Latin America. Perhaps most ominous was the precarious nature of the legal system. The wealthy and powerful lived mostly outside the restraints of law; the poor could hope for little support when they questioned the established order of things. Efforts to make changes—through demanding schools, organizing workers into unions, campaigning for political candidates committed to the poor—were often met with violence, torture, disappearance, and death.

Such was the world of Latin America. It had been that way for as long as anyone could remember, but now people were beginning to see.

To examine the truth about that world is to confront the desire, indeed the necessity, for change. If the primary fact of life is *oppression*, then the first need is *liberation* from oppression. One need not be a Christian to understand that. However, if one is a Christian, and begins to read the scriptures from that vantage point, some remarkable things begin to happen.

The first is that we discover that the world of Latin America is very similar to that of the Bible. The condition of the masses of people in Jesus' time was quite like that of most contemporary Latin Americans. The same poverty, lack of access to the rewards of power, and sense of helplessness in the face of that power were facts of life in the world of Jesus. He himself was at home in that kind of world, and his followers were drawn from its ranks.

Second, we find that the good news Jesus announced was aimed directly at the poor. The actions he accomplished were in response to their needs; his compassionate ministry was set in motion by their hunger, illness, loneliness, and despair. And those actions were firmly rooted in a specific place and time.

Third, the reign of God proclaimed by Jesus addresses *this world*. The imagery of God's city does not belong to heaven, nor is it to be found on the other side of death; it is a historical reality, lying beyond but not apart from this moment in which we live. The kingdom proclaimed by Jesus is not in the clouds but "near at hand." God's reign in human history would mean the end of the misery and hopelessness that crush the people of a whole continent.

If this is true, the reign of God must be the starting point for faith that wishes to take seriously the world to which it belongs. It follows, then, that Christians have no higher calling than to make the reign of God their own goal. If the fulfillment of God's reign remains for the future, they can at least do what Jesus did: prepare *signs* of that reign, times and places where the will of God breaks through and becomes reality.

The church itself can become such a sign of the City of God, if its life mirrors the values and priorities of that city. This is the mission that unknown numbers of Christians throughout Latin America have embraced and made their own, when they chose to place the church on the side of those whose human dignity has been violated.

The phrase, a "preferential option for the poor," first came to play an important role in the thought of Latin American Christians after a meeting of the Roman Catholic bishops held in Medellin, Colombia in 1968. That conference marked a turning point in Latin American Christianity, because it represented a commitment on the part of the church's leadership to take seriously the needs of the peoples of the Americas in the light of the Christian gospel.

Another word expressing the same idea is *solidarity*. The concept of solidarity means taking the side of someone whose situation is not our own but with whom we choose to place ourselves, accepting their fate as in some sense our own. Those who do not personally share the pain of poverty choose to participate in the struggle of the poor towards the City of God.

But why should Christians fortunate enough to enjoy earth's resources take up the cause of those who do not? Why should a church that has been identified with the status quo, endorsing and asking God's blessing upon the people and institutions that wield power, opt for a posture that may cause it grief? The answer lies in what Christians have come to believe about the *poor* and about the *church*.

Because it is taking shape among the poorest of a continent's peoples, liberation theology has never been tempted to romanticize poverty. Those who have always struggled for food, for shelter—for life itself—are of all people the least likely to pretend that being poor is easier, purer, or holier. Only those who have never lived with poverty would dare make such statements. Nevertheless, liberation theology is not unmindful of Jesus' words: "Blessed (fortunate) are you poor, for yours is the kingdom of God" (Luke 6:20).

The City of God is the scriptural image for God's purposes made flesh in human experience. It is the fulfillment of our hope for justice, plenty, and peace. As such, it is the radical contradiction of the world as we know it—and perhaps as we profit from it. The poor are those who live the contradiction most nakedly. They lack the transitory comforts and the material distractions that keep us from noticing the truth about the world. But God's will implies the reversal of the way things are. The coming of Christ hints at a world in which God "has filled the hungry with good things" and "the poor have good news brought to them" (Luke 1:53; 7:22). The privilege of the poor lies in their ability to grasp these promises most clearly; the reign of God of which Jesus spoke does indeed belong first to them.

The Christian vision of the City of God reveals, then, a perspective on both God and humanity. God is revealed as the One who hears the cry of the poor and wills their liberation and healing. God's love is poured out on those who need it most: those whose daily experience is farthest removed from the will of God for the human family. God is a God in *solidarity* with the poor. For many Latin American Christians, the God of the Bible reveals a God whose very being is a "preferential option for the poor," because a God of love does not ignore the cries of those in pain.

Indeed, the Bible dares present a God who is revealed not in power and force, but in weakness and suffering freely shared with a weak and suffering humanity. That is surely the image of the cross of Christ; it is the image of a God who promises never to abandon those who are suffering. In Paul's words,

> God chose what is foolish in the world to shame the wise;
> God chose what is weak in the world to shame the strong;
> God chose what is low and despised in the world, things that
> are not, to bring to nothing things that are (1 Cor. 1:27-28).

J. I. Gonzalez Faus, a Spanish theologian, comments on this point of view:

> Since the impoverishment of God is not for love of poverty, but for love of the poor and in order that "their poverty enrich us" (2 Cor. 8:9), God reveals himself in the poor not simply identified with them, but *with their cause.*[10]

In other words, in the life and struggle of the poor to find the world as God intended it to be, we meet the biblical God in our own history, in our own place and time.

The poor, therefore, grasp and experience something of the reality of God that is lacking to those whose lives are comfortable and shielded from pain. It is the poor who can help those who have not felt hunger and oppression to understand the real God. It is the poor who can bring God's good news to those who are *not* poor—not the other way around—as Christians have usually believed. The Latin American church has been striving to emphasize the special role of the poor in *evangelizing*—in sharing God's good news. If in fact that good news is the news of the City of God, who better to speak of it than those whose pain teaches them most clearly what it will be like when God's will is done at last?

The civil war has been going on for years. It had never come close to these mountains, but everyone had felt something of the anxiety and fear it generated.

Don Carlos remembered the last war, when the banks had closed for months, and inflation had made his money nearly worthless. He was determined not to suffer again. Day and night, he tended his coffee plants; when his neighbor developed cancer and needed to make the trip to the city to see the doctor, he was able to buy his land and even hire his neighbor's sons as day laborers. Small as it was, the minimum wage that existed on paper was far more than Don Carlos intended to pay.

When the war was over, Don Carlos kept on working. His lands stretched beyond the hills on the horizon. At times, his son spoke to him about the conditions of his workers. Once Don Carlos lost his temper. "If you don't like the way I run things, why are you eating at my table?" His son stormed from the house. Don Carlos never saw him again. There were rumors he was working to teach the peasants to demand their rights. At night, Don Carlos slept fitfully, protected by an armed guard who dozed on the front porch.

Early one morning, a group of angry men strode behind their leader towards Don Carlos' house. They were determined not to work another day without a raise in their wages. Following his orders, the guard fired a warning shot. But his aim was low. Don Carlos' only son fell dead.

Latin American Christians often recall Jesus' parable about the rich man who kept building ever larger barns to hold his assets. At the moment when he decided that at last his security was assured and he could relax, he died. Jesus used one of the strongest epithets his language provided: "Fool!" The rich man's zeal had prevented him from noticing that the wealth he had worked so hard to amass would go to others (Luke 12:16-20).

Jesus seems in this parable to be criticizing the tendency of those with access to material possessions to rely on their riches for security and well-being, even their sense of worth as human beings. It is easy to assume that our wealth and power make us important. But the truth is otherwise. Before the reality of death, we are all without resources; we bring nothing into this world, and it is certain we can take nothing with us. It follows, then, that the effort to rely for security and safety on the possessions and status we seem to control is the stuff of fantasy. No wonder Jesus spoke harshly of the man in the parable. If there is hope for humankind, it will not lie in the accidental circumstances that have given some of us more and some of us less of the world's goods.

But there is something else we must take into account when we examine the way resources are distributed in this world. If God intends the human family to share justly in what the world offers, then the radical inequality with which we share those treasures flies in the face of God's will. In other words, it is *sin*. Christians who wish to take their own scriptures seriously must reckon with that fact: *the existence of poverty and injustice in a world of abundance is sin.*

It is the poor of this world who demonstrate those two aspects of the human situation most clearly. The poor can serve as a sign of the reality of sin for a world that prefers to forget about it. The poor can also remind us that hope based solely on what we have is illusion. Just by being who they are, the poor point out the foolishness and sin of the world in which we all live together. This message is one of judgment.

That judgment is, however, the prelude to hope. Jesus did not announce the approach of God's reign without adding a call to repentance. People comfortably settled in a world of injustice will never be at home in the City of God until they turn themselves around and learn to live with new priorities. In our world, it is the poor whose very existence challenges the world to a new set of values and choices.

But it is also the poor who best grasp those priorities, since they are least distracted by the false promise of an unjust and selfish world. Who better to comprehend peace than those on whom violence falls most brutally? Who better grasps the promise of "life abundant" than those for whom life is bare?

Who can long more deeply for a world where food and shelter are distributed justly than those with nowhere to call their own? The poor, because they are poor, are in a position to hear and believe the promises implicit in the City of God. They can be our teachers, if we will listen.

If the earth's poor reveal the way the human family stands before God, they also define the choice for the Christian church. In Matthew's gospel, Jesus asserts that our relationship with him—and hence with the God made flesh in him—depends upon how we relate to the world's most needy: "As you did it to one of the least of these who are members of my family, you did it to me" (Matt. 25:40). Paul developed the same idea by describing the church as a community that lives as if it were already under God's reign. The church as a sign of the City of God practices the values of that city in its own life. It is therefore a beacon illuminating God's will for the human race.

Liberation theology has helped Christians in Latin America come to grips with the practical implications of that point of view. Countless base communities have wrestled with how they can best embody God's demand for justice and peace when the world around them is imbued with violence, bloodshed, and indignities of every kind.

One concrete conclusion many have drawn is that Christians cannot remain neutral in the struggles for dignity and freedom that are convulsing the American continent. Some have decided they cannot stand aloof from the revolt against the military and political dictatorships that rule many countries. Others, bound by their desire to avoid more violence, have sought to work towards a more just society through new forms of economic and educational structures. They have created agricultural and craft cooperatives, taught families to feed and clothe themselves, and above all have affirmed the dignity and worth of human beings who have never before heard such a message. They have striven in their base communities to over-come the ancient inequalities that have valued men over women, clergy over laypeople, and persons of means over those with nothing. In doing so, they have repainted the portrait of the Latin American church.

But the base communities are not the only segment of the church in Latin America that wrestles with its identity as a sign of the City of God. The church's institutions, allied so long with the rich and the powerful, have been shaken by the call to put themselves at the side of the people's struggle for human free-dom and dignity. Bishops, priests, and nuns—those traditionally identified with the church's structure—have attempted to take the side of the poor and live out the preferential option to which they feel themselves called. In doing so, they have placed them-selves in danger and many have been killed. Six Jesuit priests, known all over the world for their defense of the rights of the poor in El Salvador, were brutally tortured and murdered late in 1989. But they were not the only victims; a poor woman who cared for their household and her daughter were also victims of the same murderers, joining the countless Christians, clergy and laypeople, who have given their lives in the service of the City of God.

Not all Christians in Latin America agree with their col-leagues who place themselves at the side of the poor. Not all are willing to give up the position of pseudo-privilege that comes with allying themselves with the status quo. Not all are pre-pared to face the possibility of torture and death that can be the price of challenging the powers that be. Not all understand what Christian faith has to do with justice or freedom. Centuries of preaching and piety that reduced faith to a private and "heavenly" reality have taken their toll.

In villages and slums all over the continent, however, the promise of the City of God is bringing hope to Christians who have no hope. The powers who feel the challenge react in the way that Herod responded to the birth of the Messiah: they set out to kill the dream and the dreamers. But just as the Roman emperors discovered that death did not destroy the Christians' hope, the church in Latin America is learning to stand as a sign of God's city even in the face of death.

QUESTIONS FOR REFLECTION

1. Why does the author say that "the existence of poverty and injustice in a world of abundance is sin"?

2. Why do many Latin American Christians believe that God takes the side of the oppressed? What does the phrase "preferential option for the poor" mean for you?

3. How do you think having to struggle for survival would affect your Christian faith?

4. What can poor Christians teach Christians who are not poor?

Chapter 7

ON THE ROAD AGAIN

*T*here were eleven of them in all: the pastor and ten regular members of the Friday morning Bible study, people whose circumstances permitted them the luxury of gathering weekly. There was a retired insurance executive; a university professor who scheduled her classes to keep the hour free; a real estate agent; and several widows who were careful to make sure that they kept themselves busy and alert. The seriousness of their commitment was reflected in the attention their pastor gave to preparing their weekly meetings.

It was the pastor who began the session. Soon a volunteer was reading the passage from Matthew's gospel that had been assigned for their discussion.

> "Do not think that I have come to bring peace to the earth; I have not come to bring peace, but a sword. For I have come to set a man against his father, and a daughter against her mother, and a daughter-in-law against her mother-in law; ... Whoever does not take up the cross and follow me is not worthy of me. Those who find their life wilL lose it, and those who lose their life for my sake will find it." (Matt. 10:34-35, 38-39)

As the reader concluded, a profound hush fell upon the pastor's study.

In the end, it was the pastor who broke the silence. "Well, we've heard what Jesus is saying to us in this reading. What is our response?"

The professor was the first to speak. "I don't see how we can take these words seriously as something Jesus actually said."

"Go on," the pastor encouraged her.

"Well, we all know that Jesus' teachings were passed on by word of mouth for years before they were written down. You've told us that yourself."

"Yes," the pastor agreed. "I have, because I believe it's true. But why do you believe these words can't be authentic?"

"Well, it's obvious." It was the insurance executive. "Of course Jesus didn't come to bring conflict. He came to bring peace, the peace that passes understanding. If Jesus didn't come to give us peaceful hearts, what good does he do us?"

"Jim's right." The speaker was a neatly-dressed woman of late middle age. "When my daughter went off and lived in that hippie commune years ago, she used to tell me she was following Jesus better than I was, even though she never went near the church. She used to tell me I was a hypocrite and criticized every word I said. Those were terrible times, and I certainly don't think Jesus had anything to do with the trouble we had. But when I prayed to him, I remember how I always felt better—you know, calmer, more peaceful. That's why I'm sure Jesus would never have said anything like this."

"Let me tell you about an article I just read," said the pastor. "It was written by a missionary just back from South America—Peru, I think it was. He happened to mention this same passage, but he used it to explain how some of the people in the village where he was working have experienced their faith. He wrote how they had been struggling with their land-lords, and were threatened with the loss of their land if they didn't stop. People have even been beaten; and now, the village is divided between those who want to keep on fighting for their

rights and those who are afraid. He said that even good church families are divided on what to do next."

"*Well, that may be true in Peru,*" *said one of the group,* "*but it certainly couldn't have anything to do with us.*"

A century and more of biblical scholarship has helped modern, literate Christians read the scriptures critically. The study of biblical forms and sources, and how stories are transmitted from person to person, has enabled us to understand much more clearly the human element implicit in communicating the good news. Most of us accept the fact that the Bible is not only God's word, but also a profoundly human document. The questions we ask of the Bible are, perhaps inevitably, phrased in the attitudes and concerns of our world. Modern Christians in our setting are often most concerned with "what *really* happened."

As we have become painfully aware of how different our questions are from those our ancestors were asking, the value and authority of the Bible have receded for us. Though we continue to read it in our worship, we often feel isolated and untouched by the situations and assumptions of its stories. Many Christians would agree with Anglicanism's assertion that the Bible is the "rule and standard of faith," but they might be hard pressed to explain in what sense that phrase is true. More likely, we evaluate the Bible critically by what our culture tells us is possible or likely.

The rediscovery of the City of God as the focus of their hope has given Christians in Latin America and other parts of the world a renewed faith. Most of all, it has led them to orient their faith towards a future in which the values of God's city are real. That is why the perspective of Latin American Christianity offers us a very different way of approaching the Bible. It prefers to begin with the ways in which our world and the biblical world are *alike*, not different. And it reads the biblical stories, legends, and poems not to find what is still believable, but to seek ways in which light can be shed on the misery that Christians of the first and twentieth centuries suffer in common.

When we read the Bible in this way, questions of "what really happened" are ultimately much less important than the revelation about God and God's people the stories reveal. We can read the Scriptures as the unfolding story of the relationship between God and the human race as we live through our history. Tales, events, encounters become *signs* of God's purpose for the creation, especially the human dimension of that creation. We need not be sidetracked by different images of the universe or of nature, or any of the traps that so often throw up obstacles to modern Christians. If we read the Bible as God's story of humanity's relationship with a God of love and justice, we will be more interested in the implications of that relationship for our own story. And we will interpret our story with the priorities of the City of God.

Such a rediscovery could orient American Christians toward a future that gives meaning and hope to our life. We have noted that Jesus warned his followers of the need for a change of direction if they were to embrace the goal of God's city. In the same way, American Christians who are serious about embracing that goal must be prepared to see and act in new ways. A radical reorientation of our faith is called for. In this chapter, we will consider what that change in direction would mean for Christians in our society and culture—that is, for ourselves. Nothing less will serve to reorient Christians who have lost their way. Until we learn again to base our faith on those priorities, the hard bedrock on which the biblical vision is constructed, the scriptures will remain for us a trivial document.

If the Bible is correct in revealing the purpose of human life, we are called to live in harmony with God—by living in harmony with our neighbor and with the whole creation. That harmony is the result of seeing ourselves as we really are, dependent for life and all that supports life, bound together in an unbreakable bond with the human race and with all the created universe. Life is both God's greatest gift and the greatest challenge we have been given.

The harmony implicit in the word *shalom* cannot exist unless we choose to embrace the goal of justice. Biblical justice depends upon seeing each living soul as God's creation, worthy of infinite respect. The biblical viewpoint never accepts misery, hunger, degradation, or abandonment as acceptable aspects of the human condition. Apathy in the face of such suffering would be unthinkable for anyone who sees the truth that each of us is a reflection of the very being and glory of God.

If we American Christians are to find our way towards God's city, we must begin by making ourselves familiar with its contours, its reality. What, indeed, does the human community look like when the values of God's reign are put into practice? Awareness of that biblical vision is the first step towards making it our own.

But how, exactly, can American Christians learn, not only to know about the City of God, but also to make its values their own, to claim it as their home? We only put those values into practice when we learn to experience our life in the context of a scriptural framework. Here again the experience of Latin American Christians can be of use to us.

In Latin American base communities, the Bible is the primary point of reference and the chief content of reflection. But their style of Bible reading emphasizes the *concrete* nature of the biblical material. The scriptures are approached as stories that will reveal meaning and purpose when they are read from the proper perspective. No one supposes that they are abstract pieces of literature, but narratives about real human beings facing actual dilemmas and situations. In the setting of the base community, the biblical stories are read in light of the experience of the readers, and are allowed in turn to illuminate that experience. Struggling against seemingly impossible odds becomes a reliving of the story of David and Goliath, for example; or the threat of exile and prison is held up to the memory of Peter and Paul as their story is told in the Book of Acts.

But why should we expect Christians at ease in more prosperous settings, who might seem to have everything to gain from accepting the status quo, to choose instead a style of living that will inevitably cost them their comfortable position? The answer lies in what we believe about God's good news.

His clothing, his speech, even the way he walked betrayed his background. He was a lawyer, articulate and familiar with the ins and outs of the religious law. He was used to being an authority, at home with providing answers and advice to those who recognized his abilities. Perhaps he was intrigued by a country preacher who seemed so wise—or was it in order to reveal the inadequacies of Jesus' teaching that he was moved to ask a question?

"Rabbi, what shall I do to inherit eternal life?"

How can I be sure that when God's reign is upon us, I will have a share in it? The question in itself is a natural one. If the Jewish people had been waiting for so long for God's reign to appear, believers could not be blamed for wanting to make certain they would be on hand to appreciate and enjoy it.

And like any rabbi, Jesus responded with another question. "What is written in the Law? How do you read it?"

"You shall love the Lord your God with all your heart, and with all your soul, and with all your strength, and with all your mind; and your neighbor as yourself." No one could quarrel with that response; it was the summary of any Jew's obligations as a child of the covenant.

Jesus approved of this answer. "Do this, and you shall live." Faithful obedience to the covenant is the reign of God.

But the lawyer was not entirely satisfied. "And just who," he asked, "is my neighbor?"

The tone of the conversation changed at once. Now the lawyer had betrayed his real interests. He was not interested in fulfilling the covenant; he wanted to know the minimum requirements for entrance into the City of God. Behind his questions lurked the desire to do only what was necessary, as if his keeping of the rules had as its sole purpose his access to God's city. The lawyer was not really interested in faithfulness, or obedience, and certainly not in love; instead, he was attempting to negotiate with God, bargaining to find the lowest price at which to buy his way into God's reign. Jesus, of course, understood immediately. Once again, he gave no answer, but only told a story (Luke 10:30-37).

A man was going down from Jerusalem to Jericho, and fell into the hands of robbers, who stripped him, beat him, and went away, leaving him half dead. The broken, bloodied victim lay at the side of the road, giving no indication if he were dead or alive.

Now by chance a priest was going down that road; and when he saw him, he passed by on the other side. So likewise a Levite, when he came to the place and saw him, passed by on the other side.

It is not surprising that these two religious officials should shun the body they saw at the road's edge. Jewish law decreed that touching a corpse renders a person ritually unclean, unable to perform his religious duties until duly purified. Taking their obligations to God seriously meant that they must not risk defiling themselves by approaching a man who, Jesus assures us, was at least "half dead."

And yet, there is surely a catch in the story at this point. Israel's law always understood that duties to God and those owed to other human beings are part of the same covenant. How could these figures of importance and, we presume, piety draw a division between what they owed to God and the need of the man who might, after all, still be alive? The form their religion took might serve to ensure their purity, but it certainly was of no value for the man who was lying unconscious in the road.

> But a Samaritan while traveling came near him; and when he saw him, he was moved with pity. He went to him and bandaged his wounds, having poured oil and wine on them. Then he put him on his own animal, brought him to an inn, and took care of him. The next day he took out two denarii, gave them to the innkeeper, and said, "Take care of him; and I will repay you when I come back whatever more you spend."

For the lawyer and others who were listening to Jesus, this was a disturbing turn to the story. Samaritans, they knew, were perhaps the most despised of all among Jesus' contemporaries. Descended from the Jews, they had intermarried with other people and adopted non-Jewish rituals. Not only had they abandoned the Temple in Jerusalem, they also presumed to copy Jewish rites in their own shrines. Samaritans had distorted the traditions of their ancestors and scorned their God. Jews considered their touch was as defiling as contact with a corpse.

But in Jesus' story, a Samaritan is the instrument of compassion, mercy, and healing—that is to say, a sign of the reign of God! That is the shocking, the outrageous twist he gives in responding to the lawyer who wants to know the minimum requirements for entering God's city.

Within the context of Jesus' story, there are other elements we should notice. The Samaritan, as agent of healing, must approach the victim without knowing how his intervention will be received. Supposing the beaten man to be Jewish, a Samaritan could not know in advance whether his ministry would be welcomed or scorned. The victim might very well have reviled him: "Get out of here! How dare you touch me!"

The point of view of the man at the side of the road is also important. He has been stripped of everything he has, including his ability to care for himself; his condition is indeed critical. But the figures who represent the institutions that order and govern his world do nothing for him. Their concern for their own situation keeps them from being able to do anything for the beaten man.

And now, his well-being—his *salvation*—depends upon his willingness to accept help from someone whom he has always scorned. The injured man's fate—his very life—depends upon his willingness to recognize that a Samaritan can give him what he cannot get for himself. That is the most astonishing aspect of this story. It is a matter of life or death whether we can accept that those we have despised or ignored may have something we need desperately—may have something that can save us.

I am convinced that Jesus' story of the good Samaritan is crucial for understanding how we stand with regard to God's reign. And we must note that the story can be good or bad news, depending on where we stand and how we hear it.

There is a sure sound of judgment in the telling of this story. Those figures who define themselves by their authority, dignity, and piety are totally removed from its saving action.

They are irrelevant; worse, they are condemned as false priests, unfaithful stewards. The word that is such good news to the man lying at the side of the road is a word of judgment for those whose faith has made them self-important and removed them from the needs of those around them.

The story is good news as well to the Samaritans of this world—those whose station in life condemns them to be over-looked, condemned, or considered of no value. They discover that, from Jesus' point of view, they are the ones who bear the news that God's love reaches to those who need it most. Not only is their dignity affirmed, their worth as God's children is celebrated; they become *agents* of the gospel, incarnating the love that seeks out and heals the world's victims. The Samaritan is the one who acts on God's behalf, and in doing so, reveals himself as *God's image*. He also reveals his own value, because one who is thought to be nothing turns out to be the hands and heart of God. Salvation comes by the hands of someone presumed to be without worth.

Then there is the man lying battered in the road. In the moment of his crisis, he had nothing to stand on—no resources to save him from his plight. He had discovered the essential poverty of the human condition: the truth that he was powerless to save himself. The story is good news for him, insofar as he accepts his need and the ministry of one he had scorned.

Now Jesus turns again to the lawyer who had challenged him. "Which of these three do you think was a neighbor to the man who fell into the hands of robbers?"

The lawyer responded, "The one who showed him mercy."

Jesus has turned the lawyer's concern upside down. He had wanted to know what he must do; Jesus tells him the story of a man beaten, robbed, and left for dead. The rabbi must identify, not with the Samaritan, but with that victim. He must learn to see how hopeless his condition really is, how futile and ultimately death-dealing is his longing to pay the minimum necessary to inherit God's reign. He must learn to see how others, who would appear to be without value, understand God's love far more deeply than he. And he must come to understand that it is through those he has despised that he will learn how much he has already received from God.

The lawyer is not in the position of a bargainer at all; God has already poured out his blessings in abundance, while he was trying to figure out how to buy them. The story is, in the end, a shocking parable about *grace.* Citizenship in God's city is free, but we have to accept that it will come to us from those who look neither wise nor powerful nor blessed.

Ironically, Christians who have experienced scorn and disdain from the world around them are much more likely to grasp the message of Jesus' parable than those who are more at home with the world as we know it. Christians in prosperous settings have customarily read the story of the Samaritan as an example of "what we ought to do for" those in need. Such an attitude betrays our confidence that we are still "in control" of the situation, wondering—like the lawyer—what we must do to earn God's favor. It rarely occurs to us to identify with the wounded victim.

But Jesus insisted that he is of use only to those who recognize their neediness—their brokenness—and that they will grasp his power to save them only when they are prepared to accept healing at the hands of those they have scorned. In the end, Jesus himself is the "good Samaritan"—Isaiah's "despised and rejected" victim, who "did not regard equality with God as something to be exploited, but emptied himself, taking the form of a slave" (Phil. 2:6-7).

Willingness to read the Bible from the viewpoint of the world's victims is really a test of whether or not we have grasped the truth of Jesus' parable—and how Jesus makes himself known to this world. Only this perspective can guarantee that we will grasp the profound promise of God's reign.

In the pastor's study, the conversation was continuing. One of the people who had not yet spoken took the floor.

"Ruth, you know, I wonder if what happened between you and your daughter doesn't have something to do with this Bible reading. Maybe there's something here we're missing."

"Whatever can you mean?" Ruth's voice was cold, uncomprehending.

"Well, I know your daughter was hard to take when she was being so critical of you and everything you stand for. But I went through the same thing with my children, and I decided that they were right."

"Go on, Agnes," one of the others encouraged her.

"We had been members of the racquet club for years, and we'd never paid any attention to the fact that they had all those rules about who could and who couldn't belong. I'd always thought they were just silly, but of course they were much worse than that. They hurt people; they pretended that some of us "counted" and the rest were somehow beneath our attention. When we were planning Terry's wedding, she told us she didn't want the reception there because some of her friends would feel uncomfortable. The other children backed her up. In the end, we had the reception in the back yard. At the time, my feelings were hurt, and I remember telling them that when they got older, they'd understand; but in the end, it was I who needed to understand.

"We resigned from the club not long after that. It was really hard for me to admit that the young people were right. I suppose I'd never taken their opinion very seriously; I always thought only adults knew the ways of the world. Well, maybe we

know its ways too well. I've never really thanked the children for teaching me what it could be like. Maybe I should."

"It seems to me that Agnes has put her finger on something very important here," the pastor observed. "Behind the struggle she had with her children, there were some really important issues and values at stake."

"You're right." The college professor interrupted, her face animated. "When Jesus says he has come to bring conflict, he isn't happy about it; he's stating a fact of life. Of course, if we take his message seriously, there will be trouble. I suppose he could very well have said those words after all."

"And they have just as much to say to us as they do to Christians in Latin America, even if we live in very different circumstances."

Learning from the voices of those we seldom take seriously is not limited to the Christians of the Third World. Reading our lives in the light of the biblical story is not an exercise only for *campesinos* and street people. The base community provides a setting for poor Latin American Christians to relate their lives to the history of the people of God. But the same experience can happen whenever Christians gather to hear that story and allow themselves to be touched by it.

Doing so almost inevitably requires that, like the man rescued by the Samaritan, we admit that we also need to be healed, changed, and redirected. Like a mother who learned about justice from her own children, we will almost certainly find ourselves learning from those who have been grasped by the biblical promise of God's reign. The experience of opening ourselves to the values of the reign of God as they are communicated in the Bible places us in circumstances where we will be willing to hear good news from those we seldom take seriously.

Who among us has experienced most clearly the human cost of injustice, power misused, wealth flaunted, private wishes courted over shared need? Who if not the poor—victims of a world whose values are the values of death?

And who can be the advocates of life, if not those for whom life comes most dearly? Who can show the world the possibility of the City of God, if not those who long for it most deeply?

If we listen to their reading of God's history, we will come to see the power of God's promise: the astonishing vision of the human family living in justice, with all its miseries and inequalities done away.

The struggle for a new kind of world is itself a life worth living. Perhaps if we listen to those who know that best, we will come to believe it.

When we do, we will have begun to find our way.

QUESTIONS FOR REFLECTION

1. If Jesus were telling the parable of the Good Samaritan today, whom might he choose to fill the role of the Samaritan? Why?

2. Have you ever been challenged or taught by someone you seldom took seriously? How were you changed by the experience? How did your attitude towards that person change?

3. What resources can serve the function of "base communities" for Christians in the United States?

Chapter 8

BELONGING AND NOT BELONGING

"*M* rs. Davis! Mrs. Davis!"
The voice at the door was unmistakable. The years had failed to take away the accent of this Vietnamese man who had arrived, penniless and terrified, as a refugee from his own country.

Larry and Carol Davis had served on the sponsoring committee that brought Trung Chin to their community. They had been the ones who helped him find an apartment, hired him to mow their lawn, tutored him in the mysteries of immigration rules and Social Security. When his wife arrived several years later, it was the Davises who hosted the party to welcome her. They were pleased to be named as godparents when a daughter was born. Now Carol Davis recognized the anxiety in Trung's voice as he called from the porch.

"Mrs. Davis! Something bad has happened at my house."

"Come in, Trung. What's the matter?"

"The people from the city came to our building this morning, and they told my wife we must move."

"Good Lord, Trung, why?" Carol was aware of how hard it was to find cheap housing. Even after many years of hard work, the Chin family's income was painfully low.

"They say my house is not safe."

Carol was surprised; she had not seen the Chins' apartment for several years. True, it was small and dark, but the family had always been proud of their home, and it had seemed adequate, if hardly lavish.

"They say the landlord had two years to fix the building, but he did nothing. They say we all must leave because electric wires might cause fire."

"All right. Let's go and see this problem."

Carol could feel her anger rising. How could a family like Trung's, honest, energetic, ambitious for their children, be facing eviction through no fault of their own?

They stopped in front of a house that had been left unpainted for so long they weren't sure of its color. Heading for the door to the back stairs, Carol was appalled. Surely the stench that filled her nostrils had not been there on her last visit? Somewhere a baby cried; a woman's voice responded with a curse.

"Trung, you will have to speak to your landlord."

"Oh, no! I can't do that."

"Of course you can. Why not?"

"All landlords from this neighborhood know each other. If I talk back to him, I will not find another place to live."

Carol nodded slowly. She had forgotten much of what Trung and his family had taught her about the ways of the world, but not quite everything. Her face stiffened with resolve. "All right, Trung. This sounds like something for the church to know about. Let's see what we can do together."

When Christians like Carol and Larry Davis allow themselves to see with the eyes of those who suffer most at the world's hands, they come face to face with the tension between living in the creation as it is viewed through the eyes of faith and seeing the world as it is. As Christians, they also hear the words of a Christ who urges us to refuse to allow the world as it is to have the last word. It would be easy to shrug our shoulders and say, "That's the way things are," but that is not the way of faith.

Writing about this tension, Archbishop Michael Peers, primate of the Anglican Church of Canada, observed,

> It is clear that we [Christians] are not called to simple accommodation to the culture around us. The New Testament, with its reference to being in the world but not of the world, with its message about being not conformed to the world but transforming the world, makes this obvious....We do acknowledge the call of the gospel not to sink, whether in moral questions or any other, to some level of society which is below the standards of the gospel itself.

But, he cautions, resisting the least common denominator of a given society is only part of our calling. The prophetic message of the gospel also calls us to proclaim the best values of the culture in which we live, and it

> calls us to surpass them, to be a sign of that which is not only over and beyond the requirements of the culture, but that which responds to a call that comes completely and totally from outside the culture.[11]

We can identify the three elements of the church's vocation as Archbishop Peers describes them as *resistance, affirmation*, and *witness*. Each plays an important part in the life of faith.

"Jim, I've been wanting to talk to you." Carol's tight lips betrayed the casual words.

"Hello, Carol, what can I do for you?" Jim swung himself upright in his executive-style chair, and came to rest with his elbows planted on his desk. His broad, deeply lined face and heavy, dark-framed glasses made him an imposing figure.

"First, I should tell you that I'm not here on a private visit. The Social Concerns Committee from St. Martha's asked me to speak to you on their behalf."

"Well, of course, Carol. You sound serious. Tell me what this is all about."

"Jim, our committee has been working with groups from several other churches and synagogues to see what can be done about the area between Oak and Laurel Streets." Carol noticed that Jim's face was becoming set and his smile was gone.

"Yes?" The tone of his voice gave her no opportunity to relax.

"We've been researching who owns those properties. It seems to us that no one should have to live in housing like that. We're afraid there will be some terrible accident—a fire, or one of those houses could even collapse. And the rents people are paying to live there—they seem way out of line to us. The city is even going to make some of the tenants move, because they say their wiring is unsafe."

"Carol, we've known each other a long time. Are you criticizing how I run my business?"

"Jim, I didn't even know you owned any of those houses until we started on this project. But I hoped that, once we spoke to you, you'd be willing to meet with our committee and talk about how, as a town, we can do something about those slums. No one should have to live like that, Jim."

"Carol, I do have to say—this conversation is beginning to make me a little unhappy. I can't believe that someone I've always considered as my friend would come into my office and start accusing me of being a wicked slumlord."

"Jim, this is just as hard for me as it is for you. But I'm haunted by what I saw when we toured that neighborhood. There were children sleeping on the floor because their families

*didn't even have beds for them. And when they told me the rent
they were paying .... "*

*"Carol, this has gone far enough. I have no intention of
letting you, or anyone else, tell me how to run my affairs. Those
people are getting just what they deserve. What do you want to
do, put them in mansions? I'm telling you, in six months they'd
be in the same shape as those houses are now. "*

*"Jim, we're not talking about mansions. We're talking
about decent housing that people can afford, that is worthy of
raising your children in. "*

*"I'm not going to thank you for coming, but I am ending
this conversation. "*

*"There's one more thing. I should let you know that if you
and the other people who own those houses refuse to meet with
us, our committee is seriously considering the possibility of
picket lines outside your offices. We mean to deal with this
problem before another winter is upon us. "*

*"Carol, I think it's past time for you to leave my office.
Goodbye. "*

Carol's experience with an acquaintance whose "success"
depended on abusing people she cared about reminded her that
not everyone accepts the values and priorities of God's reign.
She had heard for years that Christians are called to be
peacemakers, lovers of humankind, embracers of the beauty
and goodness of creation, doers of justice. Allowing herself to
step into the world of the Chin family, she confronted the
harsher setting of crises and intimidations, ugliness and decay,
naked power and fear.

Carol would have preferred to avoid the conflict and
hostility she found herself confronting. But at the same time she
realized that once Christians raise hard questions, they face the

misunderstanding, disgust, and anger of those who profit from the world as it is. Carol chose to take the hard road; she felt herself called to live freely and fully in contradiction to that world. She and other members of the congregation learned that taking such a stance means losing forever the comforts, benefits, and support that go with being chaplains of the way things are. To embrace the values of God's reign in a setting that rejects them—in action if not in word—is to take up a posture of *resistance*, to become "no-sayers"—the first step for a church that wishes to be a sign of the City of God.

In doing so, we become the heirs of those first Christians who understood very well the need for resistance. When ordered by the authorities to stop speaking and acting in God's name, they refused. "We must," said Peter, "obey God rather than any human authority" (Acts 5:29).

It is for that reason that nearly every book of the New Testament contains a warning of the trouble to come. Those who wield power for their own ends do not give it up without a struggle. Just as the Roman night was once lit up with the burning bodies of Christians, so today the blood of countless martyrs enriches the Latin American church. People who work for peace must sooner or later confront those whose profits depend upon weapons. Those who would be advocates of justice will inevitably encounter those who grow rich by demeaning or cheating those weaker than they: slumlords, sweatshop owners, ranchers who terrorize migrant workers, politicians who use their office for personal gain. Christians are often shocked when their good intentions call down wrath or even persecution on them. We should not be surprised. Taking seriously the promise of God's city means learning to say *no*.

Such a stance identifies and names the powers for who and what they really are. One of the techniques by which unjust power maintains itself is by lying about its own identity. Repressive military regimes may portray themselves as "defenders of the peace"—as if there could be real peace apart from justice. South Africa calls the barren stretches to which blacks are banished in poverty "homelands"—as if anyone could ever be at home in such misery. For years, some areas of the United States pretended that "separate, but equal" education was the norm—knowing all the while that segregation guaranteed only to whites access to the material benefits of society. When such lies are told—and they are lies—the people of God are called to say no and to use their rightful names: oppression, violence, indignity, racism, sin.

Billy Francis was eight years old when his parents learned he was suffering from AIDS. It was the confirmation of their worst fears. Delicate heart surgery shortly after his first birthday had required multiple blood transfusions before AIDS had been identified as the threat it really was.

The first person his parents told about Billy's illness was his third-grade teacher. She was both shocked and terrified. Within hours, the news had spread through the town where the Francis family lived. On Friday night, a hastily-called meeting of the third-grade parents overflowed the teachers' lounge. Passions and fears were nearly out of control. The principal and the school nurse did their best to explain the nature of the disease and reassure their audience that other children were not at risk, but their words had no effect.

"If you think I'm standing by while my Susan catches the worst disease I can think of, you're crazy."

"What kind of family lets their child catch something like that?"

"If Billy Francis stays in this school one more day, I'm taking my son out. Who agrees with me?" The shrill, distressed voice rang out over the disorder.

"I do!"

"So do I."

"I'm with you. Let's get a petition started." The last speaker took a sheet of paper from the tablet in which she had been taking notes, and began to write. Other parents began to crowd around.

"Wait a minute." A piercing voice made itself heard over the sound of the crowd. It belonged to a short young man whose face few remembered seeing before. As he began to speak, he hesitated, searching for the right words.

"We're here because we care about our children, not because we hate Billy Francis. We love our children, and we want to do what's best for them. Of course we care about their health. But this isn't the first time we've heard about AIDS. The principal and the nurse have both told us what we know anyway. We're all scared to death, but we know they're telling us the truth. They have kids, too. They wouldn't tell us our children are safe if they weren't so.

"But there's more to being healthy than keeping germs away from our kids. Our children study history, and we expect their teachers to tell them how this country was founded on giving people a fair chance. There's nothing fair about what's happening now. How would you feel if your child were sick, and the only thing anybody thought about was throwing them out of school? Is that fair? Is that right?

"Being healthy means having a healthy spirit, too. The Francis family needs us. They need our care, our support. Billy needs his friends. I want my son to learn how to care about people when they need him. I want him to understand that things aren't always the way we wish they were. People aren't

always healthy. Terrible things happen, and I want my son to learn not to turn his back. What does it matter if his body is healthy if he's turned into a frightened, selfish creature?

"If Bill Francis is forced to leave this school, I'm taking my son, too."

The speaker sat down. A profound silence fell. One by one, the parents returned to their seats. The woman who had been preparing the petition crumpled it into a ball; the sound carried over the hushed assembly.

The speaker at the parents' meeting never mentioned his faith. But his words created a moment in which the values of God's reign were proclaimed and affirmed. By appealing to the ways in which a people's traditions and aspirations reflect those values, he affirmed the City of God at a time of great fear and pain. One compassionate parent not only said *no* to the injustice, heartlessness, and fear he confronted, but he also reminded his hearers of what they themselves believed about fair play, kindness, and compassion. He appealed to the best about being a parent. Christians who look for points of contact with the best that a given moment has to offer can demonstrate their solidarity with human values, without surrendering their commitment to God's values.

If faith were a matter of resistance only, Christians might find themselves living in a ghetto—as if, by saying *no*, they were somehow above the sordid realities of the world around us. But when we say *yes* to concrete examples of human faithfulness to God's purposes, we show that we are not observers or critics of the human story, but participants in it.

As important as it is for Christians to learn to say their *yes* and their *no*, the example of the Christian community is still more important. In its witness to the world as a sign of God's

113

city, the people of God fulfills its commitment and its identity, and obeys Christ's command to proclaim good news to all people. This is what Christians mean by mission. Mission is nothing more or less than sharing the good news we believe. That good news, proclaimed by Jesus, was life under God's reign—that is, in the City of God.

When the church fails to *embody* its own proclamations— when it fails to practice what it preaches—then it collapses into irrelevance and hypocrisy. For generations, Christian churches in some parts of the United States denied black Americans access to church camps, schools, and even services of worship. Meanwhile, those same churches listened Sunday by Sunday to the prophets' message of justice and Jesus' command to love our neighbors. A church that preaches justice while permitting its community life to reflect injustice is no sign of the reign of God.

For decades, churches have expressed concern for the earth's poor. They have opened their kitchens to the hungry, their parish halls to the homeless, and have welcomed refugees from around the world. Yet when the groups responsible for investing church resources ask about the consequences of their investments—how a given company's business affects the poor—the result is often a bitter battle. "Our duty is to get the church as much income as we can," some say. "It's not to tell private companies how to run their business." But a church that declares itself allied with suffering people, while carrying on its economic life like an investment bank with an eye only to its profits, knows nothing of justice.

Only thirty years ago, decisions about the life and faith of the Episcopal Church were made by men only. Women were seated at General Convention for the first time in 1970. The ordination of women to the priesthood and episcopate has created sporadic schisms, the threat of full-scale division, and stern warnings from the Vatican that our ecumenical progress is threatened. In the face of such dangers, some people urge caution in opening the church's leadership to women. But a church that reads in its own scriptures that in Christ there is neither male nor female, while continuing to relegate women to second-class status, forfeits its witness.

Over the years, Christians have dedicated the best of their creativity to God, and the results have enhanced the beauty of our places of worship. Art, architecture, and music have become so much a part of our tradition that it is difficult to imagine a church that ignores them. Yet the glorious setting of our liturgy can distract us from the world around us. It is possible to praise God and forget God's priorities, as if worship took us away from the world altogether. But when a church's worship ignores the pain of the world around it, that church has nothing to say either to God or to humankind.

The church as a community committed to the values of God's reign can take steps to guarantee that all people are welcome in its ranks—especially those whom the world degrades or despises. It can demonstrate its priorities by the ways it earns and spends its money. It can guarantee that men and women are equally valued and respected as ministers and leaders, and lift up the world's pain in offering to God for healing. When it does, the church becomes a powerful sign of God's city in the midst of a world a long way from home.

Merely existing as a sign of that city does not completely fulfill the promise, however. Christians are also called (as Jesus was called) to *create* signs of promise.

Jesus proclaimed the values of God's reign by healing the sick, feeding the hungry, creating joy and celebration, forgiving sins, and embracing the world's outcasts. Most of all, he proclaimed the reign of God by confronting the powers that killed him, death being the inevitable outcome of his decision to choose life. That choice was the acting out of his love, the motive for accepting the cross. Each of those moments in some sense required struggle for Jesus— against sin, against the power of evil, against the world that creates outcasts and forgotten people, against the energies and agents of a political system that acknowledged no power greater than its own.

A church that wishes to live by the values of God's reign will also find itself committed to creating signs that embody those values and make them real and concrete. It will be a healing church, a forgiving church, a feeding church, an embracing church, a celebrating church, a church prepared to confront the powers that contradict the reign of God. And it will be a church at the side of those who endure those powers.

When Christians in Latin America speak of "the poor," they know the reality they are speaking of. The buffers that more affluent societies erect to hide the naked truths about themselves are mostly absent. Christians in nations like our own can, if we wish, shield ourselves from the truth, but the Bible's definition of the poor is as clear as its attitude towards them. The poor are those who are in need of the stuff of life: an adequate diet, decent housing, proper health care, suitable education, or protection from assault and violence. They are those, in short, who have no access to the "life in abundance" that is God's gift and desire for the human family. Scripture's attitude towards the condition of the poor is one of outrage:

> Ah, you who make iniquitous decrees, who write oppressive statutes to turn aside the needy from justice and to rob the poor of my people of their right, that widows may be your spoil, and that you may make the orphans your prey! (Isa. 10:1-4)

> Truly I say to you, as you did not do it to one of the least of these, you did not do it to me. (Matt. 25:45)

The poor are those who are victimized by the ways of the world in which we live, and whose victimization is an affront to God and hence to the church. They provide, therefore, the primary agenda for the church's mission in this place and time (as in most places and times). If American Christians wish to live as citizens of the City of God, we must choose solidarity with the poor as the necessary process by which we act out that citizenship.

The mission of Christians is to proclaim what Jesus preached: the reign of God. He announced that this reign was becoming concrete in history, and that must surely be our mission as well. The church preaches the reality of God's promises and the hopes for this world to which they give birth. We believe that in the scriptures, in the life, death, and resurrection of Jesus, and in our own experiences of salvation we know something of the heights to which all human beings are called. Our mission, then, is to share that possibility.

What Christians have to offer is a hope and a community through which that hope is nurtured and served. We do not preach a salvation that removes human beings from the world, nor is our emphasis on the well-being of each individual soul (though we respect and care for each person as the gift and image of God). We proclaim the possibility of a new kind of world, coming from God and shedding hope on the whole earth, and we invite any and all who wish to share that hope to join us. That is the beginning of the church's mission.

But the content of this vision is not limited to Christians. We believe that its message is rooted in God's will for us, but we do not limit it to those who call themselves by Christ's name. Christians have no monopoly on justice, or peace, or the dignity without which God's will can never be accomplished. We can, therefore, work with all who share these hopes. We are set free from the necessity of making sure that each and every person thinks and understands reality exactly as we do. We recognize as fellow travelers on the way to God's city all those who long for that city—by whatever name they call it.

The concrete, yet tentative, way in which we find and build signs of the City of God prevents us from drawing detailed maps and blueprints to follow. How we Christians commit ourselves to Christ's reign depends on the time and place we inhabit. North American Christians can be inspired by the faith of their brothers and sisters in Latin America, but if they try to duplicate these experiences for themselves, they may well overlook the opportunities their own setting offers them. Nor can we assume that Christians in Alaska and Navajoland, in the urban battleground of the inner city and the empty expanses of the Corn Belt, face the same challenges of faith.

Yet the time has come to draw some conclusions from these reflections we have shared, and to review some of the critical areas where human beings suffer among us. We can also identify specific areas where Christians in the United States who are searching for God's city might focus their faith. Where are the victims who cry out to God for justice? Which situations demand healing and reconciliation?

+Unemployment. Both federal and corporate decisions at all levels have created a crisis in unemployment. Not only can many people no longer find jobs, they often lack the skills for the jobs that do exist. Most service jobs do not provide an income adequate for a family to survive. The minimum wage, once meant to guarantee that workers could live decently, has not kept pace with inflation and is totally insufficient to cover the basic costs of living.

Volunteers are needed for programs designed to teach job and interview skills to victims of plant closings and inadequate education. Christians in a position to influence corporate decision-making can press their firms to take responsibility for retraining redundant workers and creating job opportunities in areas of high unemployment. All Christians can urge their representatives to approve an adequate minimum wage.

+*Housing.* Unknown numbers of families and individuals are without any home at all, while many more live in dangerous or degrading conditions unfit for human beings. Christians with the appropriate skills can work with groups such as Habitat for Humanity and urban homesteading projects that build or rehabilitate moderately priced housing. Christians can let their representatives know they want their government to guarantee affordable housing for everyone, while churches can band together and establish decent shelter for those unable to tend to their own needs.

+*Hunger.* Hunger is an ever-increasing phenomenon; like homelessness, it is a direct result of the widespread and often overlooked poverty afflicting millions of Americans. While unemployment and housing shortages continue, Christian churches can support food programs in schools, shelters, and senior citizen centers.

+*Education.* The quality of education—especially in large cities—frequently does not equip children for access to the economic mainstream, but condemns them instead to a life of misery or vice on the margins of society. Christians of all ages can make a difference as tutors and school volunteers in areas of urban and rural poverty. They can insist that corporations intervene through work-study programs and scholarship funding. They can elect officials committed to quality education for all. Churches can sponsor enrichment programs after school and during vacations.

+*The environment.* Americans use a radically disproportionate share of the earth's resources, while our institutions collaborate in their poisoning and depletion. In the face of this plunder, we Christians can examine our own stewardship of the

119

earth. Are the cars we drive and the homes we live in energy-efficient? Do we buy products that damage the environment just for the sake of our convenience? Do we recycle glass, paper, and aluminum? Do we vote to care for the environment and elect those who care for the earth? In short, does our life reflect what we claim to believe about the earth God has entrusted to us, and do we communicate those beliefs to those who set government policies and standards?

+*Racism.* While small numbers of persons can take advantage of individual opportunities. most blacks, Native Americans, and ethnic minorities continue to suffer from poverty and discrimination. As they attempt to address unemployment and inequality in education, Christians are also taking a stand against a racially divided society. Individually and collectively, Christians can support policies directed toward eliminating barriers of custom and tradition that still discriminate against minorities in housing, schools, and jobs.

+*Sexism.* Women are still largely absent at the decision-making level of most American institutions—government, business, education, churches. Their earning power is a fraction of that enjoyed by men. Christians who want to right this injustice can make a deliberate decision to support capable women for election to legislatures, school boards, church vestries, and boards of directors. They can work for the principle of equal pay for equal work, and encourage women working in jobs and professions formerly reserved for men.

+*Discrimination against children and the elderly.* Children in the United States are often left to fend for themselves in situations where they are vulnerable to physical and emotional abuse. The schools fail them but provide ready training in drug abuse and crime. Millions of the elderly—both in and out of institutions—lack care, companionship, and resources for coping not only with illness, but with basic needs. Frequently the elderly feel abandoned and forgotten.

Christians and their churches are in a good position to offer care and affection to children and senior citizens in ways that affirm their dignity and provide for their needs. They can also support government programs that are designed to meet those needs.

+*Drug and alcohol addiction.* In affluent suburbs and urban slums, abuse of drugs and alcohol has been endemic for many years. Its effects are felt by every age group; the cost in social and economic terms is impossible to estimate.

Churches have been instrumental in providing for addiction treatment by opening their doors to diverse groups using methods based on the Twelve-Step principle, such as AA, Al Anon, and Adult Children of Alcoholics, but much more needs to be done. Youth ministries must help teenagers to confront the *causes* of alcohol and drug abuse. Congregations might train volunteers to assist in prevention and treatment, while churches can become centers for education about the nature of substance abuse and the social evils that contribute to it.

+*The international scene.* A nation devoted to excessive consumption that is driven by constantly expanding tastes and contrived "needs," continues to foster a self-centered attitude towards other nations of the world. Policies devised to support narrowly defined American interests cause misery throughout the Third World.

Christians committed to a reordering of the relationship between rich and poor nations can express this commitment through the representatives they elect. Both individuals and churches can encourage a responsible attitude toward consumer goods, marketing fads, and the use of natural resources. Every church could be a center for heightening awareness of injustice and promoting more just international relationships.

+*Family stress and disintegration*. The stress experienced by many American families creates households where violence, selfishness, greed, and pressure to succeed distort human bonds and help produce the very stresses that undermine them further. Christian families may wish to choose a way of life that challenges these stresses. Are the activities that drive both parents and children always worth the toll they take? Are the expenditures that send both parents out to work really enriching the family's life, or simply reflecting the need to conform to the expectations of their peers? Do churches help parents pose these questions and seek a way of living that affirms both them and their children? Are children free to explore their gifts and interests, or pressured instead to mold their futures according to their parents' expectations?

Each of these aspects of "the way things are"—the facts of our life that separate us from one another—has been noted at various points in this book. Taken together, they are all the evidence we need of the truth of what Latin American Christians tell us: the healing of the world requires more than individual conversion.

This task gives ample opportunity for us all—individuals and congregations alike—to act on behalf of the fullness of life God wills for us. Some of our actions will be directed to immediate or short-term solutions, but we must never allow ourselves to forget that in the end it is the fundamental structures of our life together that must be rebuilt, not according to the values of this world, but in the service of justice. This is the challenge that calls out to Christian people, urging them to say *no* to the deaths implicit in each sentence of this litany, even as they build signs of God's city in the ruins and the wastelands.

QUESTIONS FOR REFLECTION

1. What happens when Christians actively oppose practices and values accepted by their society? Have you ever had this experience?

2. What aspects of your community strike you as *positive* signs of God's city?

3. How does your church embody the values of God's reign? How does it fail to do so?

4. What aspects of your community strike you as most urgently needing to be changed in the light of the City of God?

Chapter 9
A PEOPLE'S CHURCH

*T*he sound of the door slamming shook the house; heavy footsteps on the stairs signalled the arrival of Jeremy, their eldest. Ellen and Fred looked at each other, silently bracing themselves for a crisis. They were not mistaken; their son's face soon appeared around their door.

"I hate this street!" he shouted. "I hate everybody on this street. I wish we'd never moved here."

"Son, what happened?" his father asked gently.

"Oh, the same old thing. I was hanging out over at the Jenkinsons', and their father started teasing me about the car."

The family car had been the subject of comments before. Certainly no other household sported two bumper stickers, one critical of the United States' policy in Central America and the other reading "End Racism Now."

"Well, it's not the first time. You should be used to that by now," his mother observed.

"Yes, but then their little sister started saying, 'Jeremy's a communist' and everybody started making fun of us. I think Mr. Jenkinson believes you really are communists.

"Anyway, I got really mad, and walked out. Sometimes I wish we could just be like everybody else. Why do we always have to take on other people's battles? Why can't we just fit in with our neighbors?"

Taking the priorities of God's reign seriously is a lifetime commitment for Christians. Perhaps the gap between our world and God's city has always yawned deep and wide, but twentieth-century American Christians have a particularly challenging role. Our place and time in history provide little in the way of support. The fragmented experience of community and the exaggerated individualism of our time are "givens" for us. We experience our Christian calling against the backdrop of a culture and society whose rampant fascination with the individual issues in egocentric and greedy behavior, which tends to define and value people in terms of what they own and consume.

The chorus of pain that rises up from those who suffer among us is a testimony to the ways in which they are abused and degraded. The victims who clamor for healing signal how a Christian people on the way to God's city will shape their journey. Those victims of poverty, loneliness, and prejudice are the flesh-and-blood challenges to a church's faith here and now.

The episode we have just considered should remind us that the challenges do not take place inside our head, but where we live—on our front porches and patios, on our assembly lines and in our workshops, in our offices and boardrooms, in our schools and nursing homes. Jeremy and his family know all too well that Christians should be prepared to examine the whole of their lives in the light of God's priorities. Faithful living affects our personal relationships—how we behave towards our colleagues, those we love, those older and younger than we, those different from us, the ill, the disabled, and the dying.

The practice of our faith also affects our life as political people. Some Christians assume that politics is somehow "unworthy" of their attention, inevitably mired in sin and tainted by corruption. But politics simply refers to the way we live together in human society. As long as we live and move among the human family, we are "political" beings. The only question is whether we will permit our faith to inform and illuminate *how* we live politically.

No one who grasps the power of political decision-making to shape the world we live in—and to enhance or alleviate suffering—could fail to care about politics or take an active role in their political system. Certainly Christians who understand the challenge of their faith will reflect on the priorities of the City of God as they prepare to vote. Which candidates are committed to justice and care about the world's victims? Whose interests are served? Whose actions are likely to stimulate the creation of signs of God's city—moments of healing and hope?

Nor can we reduce the witness of our faith in the political arena to casting ballots once a year. Christians may well be called to take an active, personal role in the political process— perhaps in raising issues publically, in selecting candidates, or perhaps even in running for office themselves.

Furthermore, many political decisions are made outside the voting booth—by school boards, city councils, local legislatures. Christians who perceive opportunities for making the values of God's reign concrete will make their voices heard. Does a proposed highway destroy a cherished neighborhood, or eliminate housing for those who need it most? Would a key project bring new possibilitites to a ghetto school? Would rezoning permit the creation of new jobs? These are questions Christians will ask and seek to answer, as they act out the values of God's city and make it the goal of their life's journey.

The life of faith also affects us as economic beings. Each of us is challenged to ask ourselves, What values determine how I earn—and spend—my money? How deeply have I been drawn into the web of consumerism—with all the traps that go with it? Do the goods and services I provide through my work enhance the cause of peace, serve justice, make the world more human?

In raising these questions, we may find ourselves at a moment where *conversion*—a change of direction—is called for. During the years when the Christian community was taking shape within the Roman Empire, the church recognized that some forms of work were simply not appropriate for people dedicated to God's city. How, for example, could Christians support themselves by manufacturing idols used in the worship of the emperor—or, for that matter, serving in an imperial army dedicated to the conquest and oppression of others?

We might not agree with all the prohibited occupations listed by the early church, but it was determined to avoid compromise with a culture whose values it feared and rejected. It is time to face the hard truth that not all ways of earning a living support or advance God's reign. In our own time, many Christians have been wrestling with the implications of this fact. Workers in the development of cruel means of warfare and mass nuclear destruction have left the security of their positions because they could no longer justify their work in the light of their faith. Others, whose conflict has been less dramatic, have made similar and equally difficult decisions.

When the construction company offered Linda a job as bookkeeper, she was more than grateful. Her husband had disappeared without warning months before, leaving her as the only support of their two-year-old child. In spite of her parents' willingness to help as much as possible, Linda felt embarassed to call on them and was determined to do the best she could to take responsibility for herself and her son.

At first, her position seemed heaven-sent. The other office employees were friendly, the salary was adequate if not excessive. Her supervisor seemed personable and genuinely interested in her welfare.

But about six weeks into her job, the office manager called her into his office. "Linda," he began, "I want to tell you how happy we are with your work. Mr. Linz has told me to keep an eye out for people with promise, and you seem to fit the bill."

"Thank you," Linda replied, surprised at the tone of the conversation. "I really enjoy working here."

"I'm glad to hear that. I think we can see to it that you have a good future."

"I certainly hope so."

"Linda, you know that housing project we're building is one of the largest construction jobs in the area. I don't have to tell you that it's playing an important part in the success of this company. All of us depend on that continued success. Now we need your help. Can we count on you?"

"Well, of course. But what are you asking?"

"Linda, it's a dog-eat-dog world out there. Sometimes, if we want to get an edge on the competition, we have to cut corners and stretch the facts a bit."

"What are you telling me?"

"Oh, come on, Linda. Don't go all naive on me. I'm asking you to contribute to your own future—your job security, all the rest."

"Just how do I do that?"

"Some of the expenses you'll be monitoring aren't quite what they seem to be."

"I see."

"One of the ways we've won that contract is to quote extra-low prices for some of the materials. We'd go broke if we gave them what we say we're giving them. I'm offering you the chance to help us make sure no one stumbles on to that fact. It's not hard at all; it just requires your loyalty. Mr. Linz will make it worth your while."

Linda's unexpected encounter with corruption at her workplace confronted her faith head-on. She suspected her manager was right; she would probably never be caught, and she could guarantee a secure, comfortable, and respectable life for herself and her small son. The alternative was to refuse; almost certainly she would be replaced. She had no evidence for what she had been told; her employer had given her nothing tangible, only promises. Yet she knew that if the company were using inferior materials, the consequences could be dangerous, even catastrophic. Some day innocent people might be injured, even killed.

Linda is a Christian. She takes her membership in the church seriously. At once she began to ask herself, "Who can help me deal with this?" She knew that at the moment of conflict and decision, she was not alone.

We often assume that the great figures of the early church were such spiritual giants that they needed help only from God as they made their way through a hostile world. But a careful reading of their story in the Book of Acts tells us something different. The apostles' faithfulness depended a great deal on the support they received from their friends.

When the first wave of persecution fell upon the Christians in Jerusalem, James, John's fisherman brother, was executed, and Simon Peter was jailed. Herod, anxious to put an end to the movement he saw as a threat to his power, intended to deliver Peter to the mob. He left him in jail until the appropriate moment, but, says the author of Acts, "the church prayed fervently to God for him" (Acts 12:5).

Astonishingly, on the eve of his fateful confrontation, Peter found himself free. He made his way to the home that served as a gathering-place for the church. When he knocked on the door, the maid who met him was so shocked she left him waiting outside as she shared the news. It was to these amazed companions in faith that Peter first told how God had set him free. Only then did he make his way to safety.

The early Christians surely remembered this episode because of the importance of the prayers and concerns of Peter's companions in sustaining him during the long days of his imprisonment. We should view that support as a crucial element in Peter's ministry.

Years later, when Paul began to travel throughout the Roman Empire on behalf of the Christian gospel, he also relied on the support of those who shared his faith. When he visited Philippi, he addressed himself to the poor women who worked by the riverside outside the city at the unpleasant and despised business of dyeing cloth. When one of them, whose name was Lydia, was baptized, she willingly opened her modest home to Paul and his companions and urged them to accept her welcome (Acts 16:12-15).

Paul's letters are full of references to those who made his witness possible. To the church at Rome, he writes, "Greet Prisca and Aquila, who work with me in Christ Jesus, and who risked their necks for my life" (Rom. 16:3-4); to the Corinthians, he exclaims, "I rejoice at the coming of Stephanas and Fortunatus and Achaicus, because they have made up for your absence; for they refreshed my spirit as well as yours" (1 Cor. 16:17-18). The image of the solitary, larger-than-life hero is not an accurate picture of the apostles at all. Rather, we should visualize men and women responding to their unique challenge, surrounded and animated by a trustworthy, caring, and sensitive community—praying for them, sharing their joys, bearing their sorrows, willing to "risk their necks" and "refresh the spirits" of their companions and leaders.

Without such compassionate support, who knows whether Peter, Paul, and the other key figures of the Christian church's birth would have been equal to their task? Why, then, should it surprise us if Christians who say *no* to so much of the world around them should need the support of a community that affirms their choices and helps them bear the consequences?

A church dedicated to seeking God's city is far different from the casual, club-like environment that characterizes many congregations. Christian communities that take seriously the values of God's reign understand the nature of the struggle of faith, knowing that they must offer their members support in the hard choices demanded of them.

A congregation in search of God's city is easy to identify. In the first place, such a church takes all its members with profound seriousness, respecting the uniqueness of each individual quest and struggle. No one is a second-class member. All are treasured, heeded, and honored, because no two people are at the same place in their journey towards God's reign.

At the same time, the priorities of that reign are taken for granted. It is assumed that people who identify with the church strive for justice, want to be peace-makers, hear the cries of earth's victims. Certainly Christians may disagree about how to make those values concrete, but the basic stance of faith points the church firmly toward the City of God.

That stance determines the program and content of the congregation's life. A community of faith on the way to God's city will be intimately involved in the struggle to bring that city to fruition. It will concentrate on helping its people understand their world, constantly heightening their awareness of the challenge and opportunities that face them.

Nor will children and young people be overlooked in the formation process of aware and active Christians. All too often, even committed people attempt to shield or protect the young from the hard realities and tough choices they must face. Of course, teachers and parents, clergy and youth leaders should be aware of the emotions and sensibilities of their charges, but limiting education to the cheerful parts of the faith does not help young people live as citizens of God's reign in a hostile world. I am convinced that is one reason why so many young persons who have been raised in the church fail to understand that their faith can support them in their own quests for a meaningful and humane life.

Perhaps the clearest mark of a church committed to the values of God's reign is that the poor and those whose lives are touched by injustice are not only the *object* of the church's attention and concern, but also are an integral part of the community of the people of God. They are heard and respected for what they can teach those who have not felt in their own lives the pain of injustice. A Christian community in search of God's city eventually becomes a church in which all people are welcome, especially the poor and those on the fringes of the world as we know it.

The recovery of a style of shared faith, which has deep roots in the Bible and the formative years of the Christian tradition, is a compelling and attractive vision. Yet we must be realists, too. The more American Christians recover that perspective, the more they will encounter division and opposition among other Christians who do not share their point of view, their style of faith, or the values that accompany them. How can we learn to face that kind of conflict within the very household of Christian faith?

Latin American Christians, who have served as our mentors in recovering the biblical image of the reign of God, are no strangers to this conflict. Their experience in confronting it can be useful to Christians in North America as they search for the City of God in their own setting.

The conflict in Latin America is the product of the church's five-hundred-year history as one of the dominant structures of the region and its culture. The so-called "institutional" church continues to function in this role, but poor Christians, who have learned to act out a new understanding of faith, have developed a different kind of Christian community. It is not a new institution, but a new *way* of structuring their life together. While the emphasis of the "institutional" church is the hierarchy (the bishops and other clergy who wield power), the new movement relies on base communities of ordinary Christians for its identity. This style of Christianity, known as the "popular" church, is rooted in the experience of the poor. These two styles of faith within the one Christian church are moved by different goals and priorities.

The "institutional" church considers itself responsible for the structures that hold society together—the schools, armies, governments, and businesses without which no society could function. While those institutions affect everyone, they are in fact controlled by the wealthiest and most powerful individuals and families. The church sees itself as an indispensable guardian of the social order, guiding, counseling, and ultimately blessing the authorities that rule and govern. While Christians within the "institutional" church are by no means blind to the failures of those structures, they are bound by their common ties to work with them and defend them. From the point of view of the "institutional" church, these structures are *givens*, part of the way the world is put together. As such, they must be maintained lest chaos and anarchy reign.

The "popular" church, or the "church of the people," on the other hand, is drawn from the masses found at the base of the social pyramid: the poor of the slums and countryside, the unemployed, the homeless, the hungry. The "popular" church hears the Christian story as good news, because it provides a glimpse of hope for change; God's will is other than what people know in their daily lives. It views the structures of society not as unchanging pillars of reality, but as constellations of power, established for the benefit of a few at the expense of the many. The church of the people views all institutions—even the church itself— in the light of the City of God. It is therefore free to judge, condemn, and even struggle against the power of those structures for the sake of the values of God's reign.

The emergence of the "popular" church has caused considerable conflict among Christians in Latin America. Those who view the church from the institutional perspective are troubled by the "popular" church's willingness to take for granted the conflict between rich and poor. For these Christians allied with power, the very nature of the church depends upon its hierarchy; it is *because* the church is an institution of society that it can make its claim to unity. A movement within the church that identifies with one segment of society—the poor— must therefore be divisive and damaging to the very nature of the church.

For its part, the church of the people responds that when the church as institution allies itself with the powers of a society, it has already opted for a posture that is divisive, because it is hostile to the masses of the poor. The "popular" church argues that real unity must be based on a recognition of the diversity of humankind, and that any peace not founded on justice is not real peace, but a form of oppression.

These two styles of church were evident in Panama in the aftermath of its invasion by the United States in 1989. Although the military action was concluded in a few days, its real effect was fully known only long afterward. More than fifteen thousand people, mostly residents of the poorest neighborhoods, lost their homes and everything they had in the night of horror unleashed on December 20.

At first, Panamanians expected that they would benefit from the new government and from a generous United States, eager to foster a "democratic" Panama. Gradually, however, the tragic reality began to sink in. Neither the Panamanian authorities nor the American government intended to respond in a serious way to the plight of the victims of the invasion. High-sounding promises turned out to be gestures calculated to deflect public attention. While two hundred new police cars imported from the United States patrolled streets made dangerous by desperate people, three thousand families remained housed in abandoned schools, meeting halls, and even an old airline hangar months after the invasion, subsisting on two meager meals a day paid for by the Americans.

Those left homeless by the invasion were not silent, but their voices went unheard, until—in desperation—they turned to the churches of Panama. In a meeting with an ecumenical delegation, representatives of the victims explained their plight. "We have written letters and sent petitions," they began. "We have marched under the hot sun and in pouring rain to the American embassy, to the President's office, and to the Ministry of Housing. They promised $6500 for new housing, but how far will that go? We have no jobs. They promised us $800 per family for furniture, but that won't even pay for a stove and refrigerator. We have lost everything! Our people are peaceful; they have endured so much, and still they keep hoping. But we are at the end of our rope; we have nowhere to turn. Only the churches—the Christian people of this country—can help us. You are our last hope."

The request for church support raised many questions and anxieties. Some people were so accustomed to being part of a church allied with the authorities—praying for their success, offering them advice, enjoying their respect—that they were fearful. "What will happen," they asked, "if the government thinks we are opposing them? We are in a position to be taken seriously; let's not risk losing our advantage."

The cries for justice did not go unheard. Eight months to the day after the invasion, the churches of Panama responded. Barren fields where crowded tenements once stood were filled with people—those who were poor and those who were not, those with resources to spare and those with nothing, together in prayer and solidarity.

The leadership of the churches was present: Methodist, Roman Catholic, and Episcopal clergy, and laypeople from the churches and from the Refugees' Committee. Prayers were offered for those who died in the flames and in the chaos of flight; for families whose livelihood went up in smoke, along with the mementos of whole lifetimes; for the wounded and those driven to despair; for those whose only home is a make-shift cubicle; for the children who relive in their nightmares the unspeakable sights and sounds of the night the sky rained fire.

Many American Christians are accustomed to a church in alliance with society's powers and structures. They may even profit personally from that alliance. The more others insist on approaching faith from the perspective of God's city, the more controversy and division will erupt within the church. The coexistence of two opposing viewpoints among Christians is as much of a challenge in the United States as it is in Latin America.

In both settings, it is unrealistic to suppose that churches allied for centuries with those who shape and dominate society will suddenly renounce their position and side with the poor and powerless. As some Christians take the side of those who need them most, other Christians—as well as the institutions of power—will condemn and oppose them. The problem, then, is not how to avoid conflict but how to deal with it creatively.

The model of church unity that has best served the purposes of liberation theology in Latin America is rooted in the imagery of Pentecost. Pedro Trigo, a Venezuelan theologian, writes that liberation theology is about

> returning to Pentecost, the foundational event of the church (Acts 2) in which the unity of the Spirit expressed itself in the plurality of tongues—meaning that, in the church, uniformity kills the Spirit, which can only express itself in the variety of cultures. [12]

I believe that the basis for coexistence in a divided church can be found by adopting and affirming the model of unity Trigo proposes. Careful reading of the New Testament reveals that the unity of Christians does not depend upon a uniform understanding of some commonly-held truth. Indeed, that kind of uniformity belongs to the "imperial" church, the church protecting its status as a social institution.

The New Testament community of faith is different; there we see people who recognize one another as members of one body and who nevertheless attempt to spell out the faith in terms that respond to their own special situations, concerns, and needs. The radical distinctions between Christians in Rome and Jerusalem, or among Paul, Peter, and John, for example, should remind us that we need not fear conflict or disagreement within the body of Christ.

Our ancestors in faith wrestled long and hard with differences of opinion. The leadership centered in Jerusalem sprang from Jewish roots, and assumed at first that Jesus mattered mainly to the ancient people of God. As the good news spread beyond the confines of the Jewish tradition, however, gentiles also found their way into the church. What was to be done with them? Must they accept the law of Moses and all the demands of the covenant—circumcision, the complex dietary laws, and Jewish family customs? Were those who had accepted Jesus as the One who brings God's reign still bound by the ancient Jewish law, as the very first Christians assumed? Or was Paul right in saying that Christ's followers were no longer bound by those rules?

The multiple challenges of living in an alien society also affected the Christian community. Suppose all the meat sold in the town market was blessed in a non-Christian rite and offered to pagan deities, as was the custom. Could Christians take it home for dinner, or must they avoid shopping in such a setting altogether?

While such questions may seem far removed from our world, we can still catch something of the tension that must have surrounded the Christians in the first decades of the church. What they discovered through argument, dialogue, and reflection is that real Christian unity is plural in form. The real unity of the church does not consist in *uniformity* but in the recognition of the rich *diversity* within the one church.

To assert that there is room within the church for differences of opinion is not to imply that our values are all relative. Christians who are convinced that the City of God orients the church toward certain ways of thinking and behaving have a prophetic role within the church itself.

In order to fulfill that special function, Christians in the United States may need to consider carefully the experience of the people's church in Latin America. The kind of clarity and commitment that are called for need careful and sustained nourishment. Without the "base communities," it is doubtful if a popular Christianity would have emerged to confront injustice and despair.

In the same way, North American Christians who long for peace and are prepared to enact signs of God's reign need the intimate, long-term support of those who share their values. Small groups dedicated to shared reflection, prayer, and worship might turn out to be requirements for building a new kind of Christian community in the American setting. In such groups, the starting-point is a willingness to examine our life and our priorities as they contribute to making a new world. The resources are there: in the scriptures read in the light of the call to justice; in prayer rooted in the pain and suffering of the children of God; in the embrace of peace that promises to bear one another's burdens; and in the word and insight of the victims who are our teachers.

It is important that we understand just what kind of role such prophetic groups can play in today's church. The prophet speaks and acts on behalf of God's city, in order that people may see and turn toward its promise and hope. Christians who are convinced of the churches' failure to live by the goal of God's city are often tempted to assume a self-righteous, judgmental posture. If they do not recognize the many ways in which they themselves fail to live as citizens of the City of God, their witness becomes smug and loses its power. Instead, they must give their witness not as those who rise above the struggle, but as those who know its temptations, the tentativeness of their own efforts, and the certainty that it is God's reign and not theirs.

In the end, it is by being honest about our own struggle toward faithfulness, our compromises, and our failures that we can perhaps move others to join us on the way.

QUESTIONS FOR REFLECTION

1. How does your faith affect the way you act politically? The way you earn a living?

2. What are the chief conflicts you experience between your Christian faith and the world you live in?

3. How does your church support you in facing those conflicts? Do its programs and worship give you the resources you need? How could it support you more fully?

4. How does your church deal with differences of opinion about its mission? How can Christians live with conflict without compromising our principles?

Chapter 10
GOD ON THE WAY

I *t lasted only a few moments. The men and boys working in the fields saw the smoke rising, but by the time they arrived back in the village, the Garcias' home was a smoldering ruin.*

It had been years since a house had been destroyed by fire in this community—something of a miracle, considering that they are all made of cane and roofed with palm thatch, made brittle and dry under the relentless summer sun.

When the men arrived, Senora Graciela was sitting quietly by the ruins of what had been her family's home, tears streaming down her cheeks. Her daughter Isabel, eight years old, the one who had let the cooking fire get out of hand, was pressed tightly against her side, her body shaking with sobs. The whole village stood silently nearby, watching helplessly as the Garcias surveyed their loss.

By the next morning, the ashes had cooled enough for the family to pick slowly through them, rescuing bits and pieces of their possessions—a blackened cooking pot, a kerosene lantern twisted beyond usefulness. But the truth had already dawned on them—they had nothing. It was as if a momentary cloud descended from the heavens, and when it lifted, they were facing the world empty-handed, stripped of all they could call their own.

And then they heard the church bell ringing. It was not just the few rings used to announce the beginning of the Sunday service, but long and persistent, calling them and the others to come together. They were surprised, because they knew that the priest would not be back again for at least another month. But leaving the remnants of their home, they made their way toward the white stucco chapel that stood at the heart of their community. As they approached, they recognized the bent figure of Senor Miguel, the venerable old farmer to whom they all turned instinctively at such moments, slowly walking toward the same destination. He was wearing the plain black catechist's robe the priest had given him when he completed a course of Bible study years before—a sign that when they met this morning, they did so not as a village, but also as a congregation, a gathering of the people of God.

When the tiny chapel was filled, Senor Miguel stood to preside over their meeting.

"We all know of the tragedy that happened to our friends and neighbors," he began. "We cannot know why such things happen in this life, but we do know that we belong to each other. The Garcia family needs us. What can we do?"

With only a moment's pause, the suggestions began. "I have some clothes that my Edgar outgrew."

"We have just harvested most of our rice. We can let them have some and they can repay us when they are back on their feet."

"I will help them rebuild their house."

"So will I. And my uncle knows how to weave thatch. I will ask him to come next Saturday to put the roof on the house."

"My children and I will help cut bamboo for the walls."

When the meeting ended nearly an hour later, every family in the village had promised to help the Garcias in putting their household back in order.

Within days, the bamboo poles needed for the house had been cut and stripped. The building itself took the better part of a day; only the very oldest and youngest members of the community failed to lend a hand. Everyone else was busy, anchoring the walls in the hard earth, hauling water, cooking the meal that all would share when their work was completed. The next day was Saturday, and Tio Pancho, the only one in the area who had learned from his grandfather how to thatch a house, supervised the delicate task of weaving the palm leaves into a water-resistant roof.

On Sunday, the village gathered as usual in the chapel. Senor Miguel presided at the simple worship. As they were about to exchange the greeting of peace, Senor Garcia rose to his feet.

"Brothers and sisters!" he began. "My heart, and the hearts of all my family, are full this morning. Last night we hung our hammocks for the first time in our new house. Without you, we would still be without a roof over our head, and our life would have been empty.

"When the fire burned our home, we lost everything. We thought our life would never be the same again. We felt alone in our misery. Even God seemed far away from us, and our hope was nearly gone.

"But now we have more than we had before the fire. Not only do we have a house, but we know we are not alone. We felt the love of each person here, strengthening us. It was as if God's own love had touched us. My friends, now I know that God is indeed here among us. God's peace is with us in this village." His hand reached out to grasp the hand of Senor Miguel. The gesture spread through the congregation: "God's peace is with you."

"And also with you."

The imagery of God's reign, described by prophets and proclaimed by Jesus, provides a set of criteria by which we know when God's will is being done. We have explored some of the implications of that image for our life as Christians: What does it mean to be a people of peace, justice, and dignity?

Our passion for a renewed earth, where history is no longer a tale of misery but the celebration of human destiny, may lead us to overlook the most basic aspect of God's reign—the dimension underlying every image of what it means to live in the City of God. We find it in Isaiah's prophecy, and in the Book of Revelation. In contrast to our experience of a world in which God seems distant or even absent altogether, Isaiah affirms that when God's reign is fulfilled, God's presence is intimate and accessible; indeed, even "before they call I will answer, while they are yet speaking, I will hear" (Isa. 65:24).

In the same way, when the seer John describes his vision of the City of God, the human community as God would have it, he declares:

> I saw no temple in the city, for its temple is the Lord God the Almighty and the Lamb. And the city has no need of sun or moon to shine on it, for the glory of God is its light, and its lamp is the Lamb (Rev. 21:22-23).

Here we reach the heart of the image of God's city: the immediate presence of the living God. Both these two books affirm that the fullness of God's presence will be known only when God's reign is complete.

This awareness is the culmination of the spiritual journey of God's people described in both the Hebrew scriptures and in the New Testament. Both covenants—the bond between God and Israel, and the new covenant sealed in Christ—testify to a common belief that it is the destiny of the human family to live united to God. That was the important discovery the Garcia family made when they were embraced by their community at the moment of great loss: when we hold one another in peace and compassion, when justice is done, then God's will is accomplished and God is powerfully present among us.

Unfortunately, the history of Christian piety demonstrates that this crucial scriptural perspective has often been forgotten. In many times and places, Christians have acted as if their relationship with God was a matter of individual concern only. Indeed, nothing seems more private and sacrosanct than the way in which we stand before God. This tendency was only heightened for American Christians as their sense of community declined and gave way to the claims of individualism.

He shuffled across the room, squinting his eyes against the morning light. Sunday was always the longest day of the week; on the other days, there was work to fill the hours and leave him longing for rest. Few fantasies or troubling visions disturbed his sleep, or if they did, he had learned to ignore them. But on Sundays, there were long stretches of empty time to be endured.

Children were playing in the vacant lot outside his window. He paused, listening to their high-pitched squeals and laughter. He drew back the curtain. "Stop making all that noise!" His voice was angry, stern. But the children ignored him. "Stop that noise, I said!" This time, they glanced in his direction and moved towards the other end of the lot. The sound began again, slightly lower. He grunted in satisfaction, turned on the television, and made his way back to bed.

The sound of choral music filled the room, blocking out the children's voices. A face appeared, smiling, warm. "Good morning!" it said. "I'm glad to see you this morning. And I'm glad you've decided to worship with us on the Lord's Day."

The preacher's eyes seemed to burn with sincerity. "I have your needs in mind," he said, "the ones you shared with me in our Prayer Campaign. I want you to know that I have taken them to the Lord in prayer, and we both believe that God doesn't ever turn away from those who ask with faith. Don't you just feel God's presence there with you as we share this hour of worship?"

Outside, the children were still playing, the sounds growing louder. But he no longer noticed. The comforting eyes of the preacher—surely directed at him, seeing him, noticing him—held his attention, became almost a living presence in the room. The sensitive voice was still speaking, telling stories of prayers rewarded, quarrels settled, unexpected windfalls....And then, the screen went dark. Someone must have blown a fuse.

He went back to the window. "I thought I told you to keep the noise down!"

We can easily identify the signs of a spirituality that has been distorted and made self-centered by its focus on the individual believer. It may be marked by an emotional attachment to the figure of Jesus as a personal friend, confidant, or even lover, while utterly without interest in whatever is not readily translated into the terms of that private relationship. Such a spirituality may even expect that faith will be rewarded, either by material rewards, ecstatic personal experience, or both. And it will ignore the bonds of community, the shared dimension of faith.

Certainly the covenant with God contains a strong personal element. Jews proudly identify themselves as members of a covenant people; Christians are baptized and sealed as Christ's own forever. Each affirmation carries with it a sense of ultimate worth and dignity that cannot help but reinforce the sense that the individual human person is loved and embraced by the God of life.

But both the Jewish and Christian covenants assume that who we are before God is experienced within a *human community* of faith and mutual commitment. Both traditions testify that the union between the individual and God cannot be a private affair, but is accomplished as we are united with others. This is why the Jewish law makes no distinction between commandments that address people's relationship with God and those that speak to their relationships with one another. It is why Jesus insisted that love (respect) of God and love (respect) of neighbor are two sides of the same coin. St. John puts it this way: "Those who do not love a brother or sister whom they have seen, cannot love God whom they have not seen" (1 John 4:20).

In this world we continue to live with expectation and hope. We are citizens of a city that is still to come, in which we will know what it is to live united with God. But here and now, God's reign appears in a world struggling to be free of death. For that reason, like all the other signs of that city that we meet in the present, our intimacy with God is just that—a *sign* of what is to come. It is fleeting, transitory, and experienced against a backdrop of suffering, fear, and selfishness.

This, then, is the question for us: How can we meet and know God—the God whose city we wait for—as we make our way towards that destination?

The Hebrew people relied heavily on their ancestors as role models who could illuminate the journey of those who came after. Because their covenant with God called them to a future that remained on the horizon, many of those heroic ancestors were travelers. Indeed, the history not only of the Jewish people, but also of the first Christians (Paul, the other apostles, the great missionaries) is conveyed by *movement* rather than by staying still, rooted to one place and time.

One of the earliest figures in the Hebrews' ancestral memory was Jacob. His story lies buried deep in the legendary past, but his significance was so central to his descendants that they called themselves by the name God gave him: *Israel*—"the one who struggled with God."

The past, he hoped, was well behind him, but you could never be sure. After all, his twin brother had much to reproach him about.

Esau should have had all the benefits of his position as the first-born son; but while Esau was honest and straightforward to the point of being naive, Jacob was crafty and cunning. As a young man, he had contrived to steal his brother's birthright. Later, he tricked their father into giving him the blessing that should have gone to Esau.

Esau's reactions were as uncomplicated as his way of life. When he realized what Jacob had done to him, he resolved to kill him as soon as their father was dead. But their mother helped Jacob escape, and for decades the two brothers lived separated from one another by miles of empty desert. Each prospered in his own way; each felt, perhaps, a love for the other stronger than either pride or shame.

And Jacob longed to go back to the land of his parents, the Promised Land God had given his grandparents, Abraham and Sarah. At last he made up his mind that the time had come. He gathered his large family, his servants, and the animals that constituted his wealth, and set out for home. From far away, he sent messengers to his brother Esau to say that he came hoping for reconciliation.

"We talked to Esau," they reported when they returned. *"He says he will come to meet you, and he is bringing four hundred men with him."*

Jacob had not counted on his brother's resources; it would seem he was now a chief, and the men of the area were known for their fighting ability.

"What shall I do?" he mused. "There is no way we can defend ourselves from an army of four hundred men. The best thing would be to divide the group, and travel by different routes. That way, if Esau attacks one, the other wil get through and we will still be able to establish ourselves in the Promised Land."

The relatives and servants were formed into two groups, while Jacob prepared a gift for his brother: hundreds of sheep and goats, camel, cattle, and donkeys. These he sent on ahead, hoping that Esau might be impressed enough with his generosity to forgive him. Finally he sent his own wives and children across the river Jabbock. For them, there was now no turning back.

As for Jacob, he remained alone as the desert twilight fell. But from nowhere, an unknown figure appeared, to wrestle with him through the long lonely night. In the course of their struggle, Jacob's hip was wrenched from its socket, but still he did not give in. At dawn, the stranger was prepared to end their match, but now Jacob refused to let him go until he knew who this unknown adversary was.

"What is your name?" the stranger asked.

"Jacob," he replied.

"You have struggled with God and with human beings, and you have prevailed. Your name shall no longer be Jacob, but Israel— 'the one who struggled with God.' "

"But who are you?" insisted Jacob.

Still the stranger refused to tell his name. He blessed Jacob, and was gone.

When he had disappeared, Jacob limped to his feet and stood silently, awestruck. "I will remember this place," he said to himself. "I will call it 'God's Face,' because I have seen God face to face, and lived to remember."

The image of God preserved in the story of Jacob's struggle belongs to a very early stage of the people's faith. Yet that same people held onto the tale because they recognized in it something about God and about themselves. In a world dominated by death, our encounters with God often take the form of a struggle. We struggle against God; we struggle to know God; we struggle to find our way to God's city. Like Jacob, we know that the destination is there, waiting for us, and that we belong there, but we can have no certainty about the outcome of any skirmish that breaks out on the way. We may even emerge wounded or injured, but that aspect of the struggle cannot be avoided. To the contrary, it is so important that it gives its name to the people who engage in it. God's people are named and defined as *"the ones who struggle with God"*—Israel.

In the same way, Christians are named for One who struggled with and for God. When Jesus began to realize that he must go to Jerusalem, and there play out the conflict between God and the powers that pretended to reign in this world, Simon Peter tried to persuade him to change his mind. But Jesus rebuked Simon, calling him "Satan"—the one who tempts us to choose death—and he "set his face to go to Jerusalem" (Luke 9:51).

In Gethsemane, we are told, Jesus prayed for escape as well as for the strength to accept his mission. Both were an integral part of that moment. Jesus would have done almost anything to avoid the terror that awaited him. He shared his fear with God, wrestling with his destiny in anguish so extreme that his sweat fell like blood. "Father, if you are willing, remove this cup from me; yet not my will, but yours, be done" (Luke 22:42). Hours later he hung on the cross and cried, "My God, my God, why have you forsaken me?" (Mark 15:34)

Jesus, then, also deserves the name *Israel*: "the one who struggled with God." He agonized over accepting his role as the Servant who dies for the many. He knew the depths of loneliness and the experience of abandonment. His sense of emptiness and solitude was also an inevitable part of the journey of God's servant. He emerged eternally scarred, so that even in his resurrection his hands and side bear the marks of struggle with life and with death.

We are called by his name: *Christians*. The journey towards the City of God is a pilgrimage marked by struggle and even death. Like the children of Israel, our name includes a reminder of that struggle. But like Jacob, like Jesus, we find that at the heart of the struggle is God.

God, said Jesus, "is God not of the dead, but of the living" (Matt. 22:32). It was in the service of this God of life that Jesus lived and died; indeed, John's gospel quotes him as saying, "I came that they may have life, and have it abundantly" (John 10:10). The theme echoes throughout the New Testament. The pivotal sign of Christ's reign is his resurrection from the dead, a victory that Paul interprets as the first-fruits of a victory over all death and the guarantee that God's reign is indeed among us.

It must surely follow, then, that if we wish to encounter this God, we must seek out life; we must be servants of life. Christians have inherited a tradition that makes it possible to celebrate and cherish the life we experience as God's gift; in embracing that life, we embrace the Giver. To serve and celebrate life is to encounter the Spirit who gives life. The opportunities we will have for becoming aware of the presence of God among us—in spite of the fragmentary nature of that experience, in spite of the death that still surrounds us—will be precisely those moments when we are most single-mindedly living in the *service of life.*

Jesus' followers have always had trouble grasping this point. Because the presence of God's love in this world is often hidden, we can easily overlook it. Jesus himself once spoke of the time when God's reign would be revealed in its fullness. Many, he promised, would be invited to share in its blessings,

> for I was hungry and you gave me food, I was thirsty and you gave me something to drink, I was a stranger and you welcomed me, I was naked and you gave me clothing, I was sick and you took care of me, I was in prison and you visited me. (Matt. 25:35-6)

"Lord, when did we see you?" his friends ask in astonishment.

The question reminds us that in this place and time, God is not so easily recognizable. Jesus was meant to be the "enfleshed" God, God dwelling among us, but most people failed to see him that way. Matthew tells us that the same Christ continues to be "enfleshed," hidden in a form that makes him difficult to recognize—unless you know where to look. The purpose of the story is to remind us *where* to look—or rather, in what particular sorts of circumstances Christ is hidden.

Jesus' answer is very clear. "As you did it to one of the least of these who are members of my family, you did it to me" (Matt. 25:40). But the implications of that remarkable insight have rarely been incorporated into Christian spirituality. If we think about the passage at all, it is in conjunction with "good works," how to act out our service to God, or what we do *because* we already know and love God or Christ. But this misses part of the point. Serving the poor—placing ourselves at the side of the wretched of the earth—is not only something we do *because* we know Christ, but it is also in that act of solidarity that we *come to know* Christ. Indeed, the parable suggests that there is no other certain way by which we can arrive at a knowledge of Christ at all. *Only* the act of placing ourselves at the service of the City of God—in the act of serving the world's victims—carries with it the promise of a meeting with the Christ who is God in the flesh.

The reason is that if Jesus once "enfleshed" God, it is now the poor, those at the margin of life, the outsiders bereft of dignity and hope, who present to us the human face of the crucified Christ. These verses tell us something crucial about the God whom we are seeking. This God, once made flesh in Jesus, is now hidden among those who continue to be crucified; the God we look for is a God in solidarity with the poor. Nothing less than our solidarity will make it possible for us to draw near to such a God. Our stance with regard to the earth's victims determines how well we will know the living God.

The God of life, animated by a love that goes beyond our ability to imagine, calls a new kind of life into being. Through the human agents who have been captivated by God's purposes, a new community comes into being at the service of those purposes. Signs of God's reign appear among us, to be wondered at and celebrated. When we are privileged to grasp a moment of that reign, a corner of that City, we are inspired to long for more, and to do what we must so that that reign becomes more and more a reality.

How do we celebrate the City as we know it and long for it? In the midst of the challenges that would destroy it, how do God's own people cling to their vision and their hope?

In the darkest night of his time among them, Jesus himself provided a way. In the midst of a bitter-sweet celebration of the Passover—singing hymns of freedom while his homeland was in chains—he took bread and wine, and made those signs of life into the celebration of the City of God.

In Jesus' action, bread and wine—the signs of our life and labor—are named for what they are: God's gifts, by which we are nourished and our lives sustained. They are declared *holy*, fit to be signs of the holy God who sustains and noursihes us. Obeying his commandment, we gather in community, a holy community that itself serves as a sign of the coming City of God. We receive food and drink, and return to the world of death, strengthened by what we have received and by remembering who we are. In the Eucharist we meet the One who is life for us, and become ourselves signs of the living God and servants of life.

The purpose of such a meal is precisely that we may be able to place ourselves on the side of life—at the side of those who are victims of death. The quest for justice, the search for peace, the gestures by which we share the dangers and the sufferings of the poor and broken of the earth, are part of our affirmation of life, the *yes* in which we glimpse and even touch the God of life.

Serving life, however, is itself a risky, sometimes deadly, task. Celebrating life in the face of death is a dangerous enterprise. That is why this celebration takes place within a *community* of support and shared hope. The important role played by Jesus' friends and companions at his last supper is surely not accidental. When we act out that scene of comfort and strengthening, we do so surrounded by those who share, at the deepest level, the vision of the City of God.

Like so much of the church's tradition, the Eucharist can be put to the service of a private spirituality, in which the only thing that matters is a personal relationship with God—*my* Communion, *my* comfort in a world that seems alien and hostile. But it can also be approached and interpreted in the light of the Bible's own perspective, the City of God.

If the Eucharist is to serve and deepen our commitment to God's city—our commitment to life according to God's own purposes—we must take care never to permit our own individual feelings, concerns, and even our piety to overshadow its primary identity as the shared communion of the people of God. At the Last Supper, Jesus tended the anxieties of his followers and helped them face what was to be their worst hour. But he did so by addressing them as a community, almost a family, in spite of their diverse points of view, their quarrels and rivalries, and the private agenda each brought to their gathering.

So it must be with the Eucharist. Our faithfulness to Jesus' memory—"Do this in remembrance of me"—must begin with our awareness that we are breaking bread *together*. In that way, every gathering of God's people becomes a sign and witness of the possibility we long for. Every time we break bread becomes a time for strengthening; every time we share the cup, a moment that animates and awakens us. Any celebration of the Eucharist that does not affirm this perspective fails to do justice to Jesus' own intentions. In the words of the Episcopal Church's Book of Common Prayer:

> Deliver us from the presumption of coming to this Table for solace only, and not for strength; for pardon only, and not for renewal. Let the grace of this Holy Communion make us one body, one spirit in Christ, that we may worthily serve the world in his name.

If the church is truly acting as a sign of God's city, we may find in it a setting where our own worth is valued, where we share with others our hopes as well as our fears. We will be nurtured by faithful friends for what lies ahead, and in the embrace of that loving community, the love of God will make itself known. If we absent ourselves from that possibility, God's love will never have a chance to break through, and we will be deprived not only of a vision, but also of the strength to move towards that vision.

If we take seriously the perspective on spirituality that I am suggesting, we may well find ourselves with a new understanding of prayer. Yet we need not depart from our biblical roots, since Jesus' own prayer was framed and offered in the context of the City of God. Indeed, the prayer we identify with him makes no sense apart from the hope for God's city: "Your kingdom come, your will be done on earth as in heaven" is a cry for the fulfillment of God's will, a new earth as well as a new heaven.

The prayer Jesus taught his disciples begins with a petition for the hallowing of God's name. In the idiom of the time, this calls for appropriate reverence for the name, that is the identity, of God. But to show reverence for the living God is to show reverence for the life that is the sacrament of God's name. The only way we can show forth the holiness of God is by treating as holy whatever reflects the being and nature of God—which is all of life.

The request for food—"Give us this day our daily bread,"—also makes no sense apart from what we believe about the City of God. If God does not care about people's hunger, why ask to be fed? By recognizing the prosaic but altogether human need for food, the prayer of Jesus relates the promise of the City of God to the facts of daily life. The satisfaction of human need is itself a sign of God's city.

The prayer for forgiveness as we forgive others articulates what has already been noted about biblical religion: our relationship with God mirrors and depends upon our relationship with other human beings. The primary fact of our life as we stand before God is our need for acceptance, but Jesus' prayer reminds us that we dare not even ask for such forgiveness unless we are ready to accept others as they are. The words of his prayer make the same claim as the parable in Matthew 25 ("As you have done it to one of the least of these ..."). There *is* no bond with God apart from the bond that unites us with our brothers and sisters.

Prayer on the way to the City of God is how we orient ourselves toward the God who is waiting for us at our journey's end. The fullness of God's love for us will be made known only when God's will for the human family is accomplished. Until that day, we work and hope our way towards a future we have not yet seen. But we do not travel in silence; we sing and shout and cry with those who travel with us, confident that God is on the horizon. We are not without resources for the journey; we have traveling companions and food for our pilgrimage. In times of loneliness and fear, we are sustained by memories and hope, even when God is hidden from us.

If we live in this world as strangers, it is because we are waiting for a *new* world. If we are impatient with violence and war and injustice, it is because we refuse to believe they are the last word about this earth and its peoples. When we dare to share our hopes with God, we are following the example of Jesus, who also prayed: "Your kingdom come! Your will be done, on earth as in heaven."

QUESTIONS FOR REFLECTION

1. Comparing the experience of the Garcia family with that of the man watching a television evangelist, which is a more authentic expression of faith in the God of the Bible? Why?

2. Do you agree with the author that "God's people are named and defined as 'the ones who struggle with God' "? Why?

3. How do you respond to the author's assertion that "if we wish to encounter ... God, we must seek out life; we must be servants of life"? What does this imply about Christian spirituality?

4. Why does the author consider that the purpose of the Eucharist is "that we may be able to place ourselves at the side of life—at the side of those who are victims of death"? Does this change your understanding of Holy Communion?

A LAST WORD

We have come to the end of these reflections, but not, of course, to the end of our journey. These pages were written out of my conviction that Americans have suffered a collective loss of destiny that has left us disoriented, prey to the many distractions that threaten to keep us from our journey's goal. Our ancestors expressed that goal in terms of justice, freedom, human dignity, and equality. But they did not invent those values; they inherited them from the ancient people of God and from the followers of the One who opened their promise to the whole human race.

Seeking to reorient ourselves toward a goal worthy of a human family created in God's image, we have returned to the story of our first spiritual forebears, the Hebrew people. We have retraced their longing for a world where God's will would be fulfilled, even as we recalled their failings and disappointments. And we have placed ourselves at the side of Jesus and his friends, as they grasped in astonishment the truth that God's reign, so long expected and so long delayed, is at last taking flesh in human history. Justice, peace, and compassion mark its arrival; death is overcome and life breaks forth from the tomb, triumphant, lighting up the future with infinite God-given possibility.

Like the earliest followers of Jesus, we have had to reckon with the delay of that reign in its fullness, as we face the continued power of death to damage and destroy God's creation. Like them, we have also confronted the challenge to hold on to our dream and to live by the values of God's city, even when it remains a distant goal. As twentieth-century American Christians, we have dared to examine the peculiar challenges to those values that our own place and time present for faith. Our commitment to the dream of God's reign does not contradict the need for realism as we assess those challenges. We have permitted ourselves to hear the cries of the world's poor, to notice the hunger and misery of millions of God's children. With halting steps and gestures, we have tried to place ourselves at their side in our mind's eye, in order to take concrete steps of solidarity in the future.

The destination remains distant. Every day brings new evidence of the power of death to deceive and seduce us, to deaden our senses and our sensibility. But we do not walk alone through the darkness. We belong to a people of hope and courage, with generations and centuries of commitment and a history of bearing one another's burdens.

We journey as baptized children of God—plunged into the water that is the fount of life, to symbolize that we belong not to death but to life. At that moment, we receive our name, our priceless identity as a member of the human family and of the body of Christ. Whatever our fate in this world, we belong to God and share the image of God's creative love in the depths of our being.

We travel as a people marked with the sign of the cross, the sign of Christ's own struggle for life against the powers of death. And we travel as members of a community of pilgrims, who have embraced us as brothers and sisters, and who walk with us on the way, sharing bread and wine as signs of who we are and what we hope for.

> Thomas said to Jesus, "Lord, we do not know where you are going. How can we know the way?" Jesus said to him, "I am the way..." (John 14:5-6).

> For here we have no lasting city, but we are looking for the city which is to come (Heb. 13:14).

ENDNOTES

1. John Winthrop, "A Model of Christian Charity" in Conrad Cherry, ed., *God's New Israel: Religious Interpretations of American Destiny* (Englewood Cliffs, NJ: Prentice-Hall, 1971), 43. The quotations in this chapter from Langdon, Stiles, Beveridge, and Gladden are from the same work, pp. 100, 90, 105, 116, 84, 263.

2. Jerry Falwell, *Listen, America!* (Garden City, NY: Doubleday, 1980), 21-22, 29.

3. Robert N. Bellah, "Civil Religion in America," in William McLoughlin and Robert Bellah, eds., *Religion in America* (Boston: Beacon Press, 1966), 5-6.

4. William Lawrence, "The Relation of Wealth to Morals" in Cherry, 246.

5. Robert Bellah, *The Broken Covenant*, (New York: Seabury Press, 1976), 142.

6. Tom Wicker, "A Falling Standard," *New York Times* (Aug. 17, 1987).

7. Herbert London, "What TV Drama is Teaching Our Children," *New York Times* (Aug. 23, 1987).

8. Bret Easton Ellis, *Less Than Zero* (New York: Penguin Books, 1986), 205, 208.

9. For an excellent analysis of this phenomenon, see Gibson Winter, *The Suburban Captivity of the Churches* (Garden City, NY: Doubleday, 1961).

10. J.I. Gonzalez Faus, "Los pobres como lugar teologico," *Revista Latinoamericana de Teologia*, 1 (Sept.-Dec., 1984), 289. (Translation by the author.)

11. Michael Peers, "The Church As Sign of God's Kingdom" in *Phos* (Easter, 1987), 1.

12. P. Trigo, "Analisis teologico pastoral de la Iglesia Latinoamericana," *Revista Latinoamericana de Teologia*, 4 (Jan.-Apr., 1987), 55. (Translation by the author)

INDEX OF SCRIPTURAL PASSAGES

DATE DUE

OCT 19 1992			